THE PROSPEROUS PHD

A go-to resource for the PhD journey, *The Prosperous PhD* sets doctoral students on a path of healthy progress that helps them avoid the all-too-familiar pitfalls of program burnout and withdrawal. With over 140 pieces of insightful wisdom from expert supervisors representing forty-five institutions across eight countries, this book provides diverse perspectives to address themes of "fostering relationships," "seeking balance," and "focusing on growth," among others. The advice points to attainable goals and concrete strategies to help achieve them. These lessons are taken a step further through dozens of detailed exercises that help graduate students apply the book's principles and better their lives.

The Prosperous PhD encompasses the gamut of graduate-student experiences, tribulations, dilemmas, and decisions – from choosing a supervisor and a topic to writing up a dissertation, finding life balance, navigating departmental politics, and becoming an autonomous, happy researcher. Readers can study the book from start to finish to gain a holistic picture of the doctoral journey or select individual chapters to find the perfect piece of advice for their particular stage or challenge.

Created by a team with extensive experience on both sides of the doctoral journey – as PhD students and supervisors – this book is a student-friendly, practical guide that will propel readers toward a more prosperous PhD.

JUDY WEARING is the lead learning architect at OpusVi Inc. She holds two PhDs, the first in biology from the University of Oxford and the second in education from Queen's University.

CHRISTOPHER DELUCA holds a PhD in education from Queen's University, where he now serves as a professor and director of the Assessment and Evaluation Group in the Faculty of Education.

STEPHEN MACGREGOR is an assistant professor of educational leadership, policy, and governance and the director of experiential learning at the University of Calgary's Werklund School of Education.

THE PROSPEROUS PHD

SECRETS TO SUCCESS FROM TOP SUPERVISORS

Judy Wearing, Christopher DeLuca,
and Stephen MacGregor

UNIVERSITY OF TORONTO PRESS
Toronto Buffalo London

University of Toronto Press
Toronto Buffalo London
utppublishing.com
Printed in Canada

ISBN 978-1-4875-5214-5 (cloth)
ISBN 978-1-4875-5215-2 (paper)
ISBN 978-1-4875-5216-9 (EPUB)
ISBN 978-1-4875-5219-0 (PDF)

Library and Archives Canada Cataloguing in Publication

Title: The prosperous PHD : secrets to success from top supervisors / Judy Wearing, Christopher DeLuca, and Stephen MacGregor.
Names: Wearing, Judy, 1968– author | DeLuca, Christopher, author | MacGregor, Stephen (Teacher), author.
Description: Includes bibliographical references and index.
Identifiers: Canadiana (print) 20250291614 | Canadiana (ebook) 20250291665 | ISBN 9781487552145 (cloth) | ISBN 9781487552152 (paper) | ISBN 9781487552190 (PDF) | ISBN 9781487552169 (EPUB)
Subjects: LCSH: Doctor of philosophy degree. | LCSH: Doctoral students. | LCSH: Universities and colleges – Graduate work.
Classification: LCC LB2386 .W43 2026 | DDC 378.2 – dc23

Cover design: Tamara Hawkins
Cover image: baona / Shutterstock
Interior illustrations: Owl and plant illustrations courtesy of Freepik; book illustration courtesy of mangsaabguru

The manufacturer's authorised representative in the EU for product safety is Mare Nostrum Group B.V., Mauritskade 21D, 1091 GC Amsterdam, The Netherlands. Email: gpsr@mare-nostrum.co.uk

We wish to acknowledge the land on which the University of Toronto Press operates. This land is the traditional territory of the Wendat, the Anishnaabeg, the Haudenosaunee, the Métis, and the Mississaugas of the Credit First Nation.

University of Toronto Press acknowledges the financial support of the Government of Canada, the Canada Council for the Arts, and the Ontario Arts Council, an agency of the Government of Ontario, for its publishing activities.

Canada Council for the Arts
Conseil des Arts du Canada

Funded by the Government of Canada
Financé par le gouvernement du Canada

Contents

CHAPTER ONE

Beginning: The Doctoral Journey

This book compiles advice from the world's top supervisors about how PhD students can thrive in their doctoral programs. Written primarily for PhD students (or those thinking about undertaking graduate work), this invaluable resource aims to set doctoral students on a prosperous path of healthy progress, one that nurtures social-emotional needs and avoids the all-too-familiar pitfalls of program burnout and withdrawal.

We present a compilation of advice from exceptional supervisors who were systematically identified and contacted from around the Western world about how you as a PhD student can prosper, both within and beyond your PhD. Spanning many international contexts and diverse disciplines, the brief, pithy wisdom featured in this book is thematically arranged by chapter to promote a deeper understanding of what it means to be successful in doctoral studies. Each chapter concludes with practical strategies and tangible activities to encourage reflection, application, and extension of ideas to your own personal circumstances. Our aim in writing this book is to encourage you to actively plan for your success by becoming more mindful of your choices, actions, and intentions. Let's get started!

How to Use This Book

There is no "right way" to read or use this book.

If you are just starting out on your PhD journey – or are considering graduate work and want to know if it's right for you – review the book from start to finish to gain a more holistic picture of the doctoral journey. Each chapter opens with a short, provocative summary of the theme followed by advice from supervisors around the world. The chapters conclude with practical activities and strategies that invite you to apply and reflect on the advice in relation to your own doctoral studies. Reading the book from start to finish will give you a good sense of the doctoral journey – key milestones, considerations, and potential pitfalls – as we have sequenced the chapters loosely based on typical major stages in doctoral programs. Of course, there are instances where advice remains applicable across all stages of a doctoral program, and aspects of a doctoral program that are not included in the advice, such as examinations.

However, because we have arranged the advice thematically, you can also engage with individual chapters based on their relevance to your particular stage or challenge, be it choosing a supervisor and a topic, or writing up a dissertation. If you are facing a particular issue, you might find value in reading a chapter more than once. Engage with the advice and concepts – highlight important ideas, write in the margins, cut out advice and post it, create your own advice, read the book with your peers, talk to your supervisors about the advice. This book is your guide, so use it in whatever way propels your PhD studies.

We envisioned this book to also be a space for your active planning and reflection – think about it as your own personal PhD journey workbook. The lessons from each chapter are fortified with practical exercises that enable you to directly connect the advice to your personal circumstances through actionable strategies and activities. Many of the exercises are based on best practices and research from fields such as leadership and education. These strategies present you with the opportunity to put the stellar advice presented here into practice and advance your work in productive ways.

As you well know, a PhD requires a lot of hard work, and just by signing up for graduate studies you're demonstrating a commitment to that level of effort. Don't you owe it to yourself to make this journey as smooth and successful as possible? The fact that you're reading this right now demonstrates that you understand the value of seeking advice. Take the further step of putting effort into the exercises to develop your skills in dealing with the challenges. As the adage goes, "a PhD is about learning about yourself." We feel sure that understanding your strengths and weaknesses, and practicing healthy strategies in real time, will help you define your goals and set you on a path to a more prosperous PhD.

Why This Book?

In a windowless lecture hall on a warm spring day, I, Judy Wearing, sat for the first time in the environs that would be my academic home for years to follow. The speaker was Christopher DeLuca, then an assistant professor in the Faculty of Education, who was welcoming a new crop of graduate students. I was one of them. I was sitting directly in line with the lectern, three rows up. His brief talk was unlike anything I'd heard before: in my previous PhD experience, in the Department of Zoology at Oxford, or in my subsequent work with graduate students around the globe.

Chris spoke about us not as students with research to conduct and a dissertation to write, but as human beings who were there – in that lecture hall, at that university, at that time – for a reason. Humans whose thoughts and feelings would be inextricably linked to and embedded in our work. "Why?" he asked us, "Why are you here to do research on your chosen topic? Why you? Why this topic? Why now? But mostly, why *you*?"

Why. A simple question, but the answers that came up on the drive home as I reflected on the trajectory of my life were highly emotional. It was quite a revelation to grasp just how much my dissertation topic, creativity, meant to me as the provider of hope and companionship during the tough, lonely times I had growing up. Chris's simple question was the beginning of my qualitative research training. I have asked dozens of other PhD students the same question since, and I have been amazed at their power to bring to life the purpose of their research. Excavating such a personal connection to purpose provides clarity and motivation during those grueling days and weeks of a graduate degree.

The Prosperous PhD arose from the interactions between Christopher DeLuca, now professor and former Associate Dean of Graduate Studies at Queen's University, Canada, and Judy Wearing, two-time PhD earner, and the recipient of his sage advice. We wrote this book, with the support of Stephen MacGregor, who was initially a PhD student and is now a PhD supervisor himself, to ensure all PhD students had access to sound advice as they pursued their doctoral studies. We recognize that not all doctoral students have PhD supervisors, and that the quality of supervision varies. And so, this book provides support by drawing on the immense wisdom of exceptional doctoral supervisors from diverse universities.

PhD pursuit is on the rise, globally, in part due to what Dore[1] originally termed the "diploma disease," the increasing pressure for degree escalation across sectors. The projected growth responds to continued credentialing and heightening global competition for fewer specialized jobs coupled with a desire for increased socioeconomic status. Graduate student tuition, particularly international tuition, is also a central source of income for higher education institutes, with tuition rates increasing.[2] In short, the PhD is on the rise and greater supports are needed – including instructive and practical texts – to ensure doctoral students succeed in this financially and emotionally costly pursuit.

PhD students need advice and mentorship because graduate work is difficult. Attrition rates are alarmingly high – 40 to 50 per cent of those who begin a PhD do not graduate. The pandemic has not improved the situation. The prevalence of mental health issues is also alarming, with approximately 50 per cent of PhD students experiencing psychological distress and 33 per cent at risk of a common psychiatric disorder.[3,4,5]

Recent studies illustrate that the challenge of PhD completion and the socio-emotional strain are far from localized to a particular country or university; Evans et al., for instance, surveyed over twenty-two hundred graduate students (90 per cent PhD students) from twenty-six countries and 234 institutions about their experiences with depression and anxiety, using clinically validated scales.[6] What they found is disquieting: their study suggests that graduate students are six times more likely to suffer from depression and anxiety compared to the general population, and more than one third of participants experienced moderate to severe symptoms. Hazell et al.'s systematic review and meta-analysis of doctoral students' mental health further elucidates the extent of the issue. By synthesizing the results from fifty-two studies published between 1979 and 2018, they found that "poor mental health is a pertinent problem facing DRs [doctoral researchers]; stress appears to be a key issue and significantly in excess of that experienced in the general population" (Hazell et al., 2020, p. 24).

It is not only higher education researchers taking note of the challenges faced by PhD students. Universities and student associations are also increasingly collecting data on the graduate student experience, including both institutional barriers and potential supports. The University of California, Berkeley, for example, found from a survey of its graduate student population that about 47 per cent of its PhD students met the threshold conditions for depression.[7] A study at the University of Arizona suggests PhD students do not enter their studies with poorer mental health; rather, for many students, their subjective mental health ratings decline throughout their program of study.[8] The salient question, then, is what can be done to improve the life situations of PhD students?

Turning again to the most recent and reliable research evidence, PhD students appear more equipped to navigate mental health challenges when they engage in self-care, build and employ effective coping strategies, and have positive supervisor relationships.[9] This last factor – supervisor relationships – is a core aspect of the social environment of doctoral education, and the focus of this book. Studies more broadly link positive supervisor-student relationships to positive mental health and program outcomes.[10,11,12,13]

According to Berkeley's *Graduate Student Happiness and Well-Being Report 2014*,[14] advisors have significant influence over multiple factors related to graduate students' well-being including academic progress and preparation, finances, career prospects, and feeling valued and included in a department. These findings underscore the critically important role that mentors play in the lives of PhD students, including helping them to see beyond the immediate pangs of the doctoral process. The influence of trusted supervisors led Hazell and colleagues to describe their influence as transcendent, producing "growth, change and self-actualization, involving empowerment through knowledge, self-discovery, and developing increased confidence, maturity, capacity for self-direction and use of one's own autonomy" (Hazell et al., 2020, p. 24).

What makes a supervisor effective remains contested in the empirical literature. Every PhD student requires a unique blend of social, emotional, academic, and career guidance, and research suggests that supervisors and supervisees often have different perspectives on what guidance is needed and when.[15,16,17] Furthermore, there are myriad examples in the research of "inconsistencies and problems between supervisors and supervisees,"[18] such as the provision of dubious advice, inadequate supervisory skills, and limited opportunities to hear varied perspectives on academic life. These challenges leave many PhD students with a pressing need for guidance that is beyond their own supervisor's ability to provide. Even PhD students who have a positive relationship with their supervisor will have information needs that exceed the depth of any one supervisor's knowledge and experience.

Just like the simple question Chris asked, *why?*, we recognize that a few well-placed words of advice can have huge impacts on the lives, and research, of those who hear them. Given that graduate students need advice, and many do not have an endless supply of it at hand, we've collected the best advice from top supervisors in a diversity of fields, around the English-speaking world.

About the Advice

We have gathered a wide variety of perspectives and collected them in one book. Unlike other PhD guidebooks, which typically provide the views of one scholar or writer, this book draws on the wisdom of over seventy scholars from a wide range of geographic locations and academic disciplines. Their advice covers the gamut of typical graduate student experiences, tribulations, dilemmas, and decisions – such as nailing down a research topic, procrastination, social isolation, perseverance, and scoping a project to a manageable scale – to larger considerations such as how to stay true to yourself, becoming your own advocate, and learning how to build cathedrals.

We used a systematic process of gathering advice. We first sought the recipients of high-profile higher education teaching awards, such as the 3M Teaching Award in Canada. We then used the *Times Higher Education* World University Rankings 2020 to identify the top 250 universities with the highest "teaching" scores, as supervision is typically considered within the "teaching" category within the rankings. We systematically screened each of those institutions for awards or recognition related to graduate student supervision, mentorship, or teaching. Most universities either did not publicly share such information or did not have any such awards or recognition. We also contacted Deans of Graduate Research, or an equivalent role, and asked them to nominate supervisors in their institution who were noted for their graduate supervision excellence. As an additional recruitment protocol, we invited nominations from outstanding supervisors through a "snowball sampling" process. We further sought advice from excellent supervisors in broad disciplinary fields and geographic regions that were less represented in our initial responses. We ceased collection of advice when responses began to be highly repetitive.

All supervisors contacted were asked to answer two foundational questions. These two questions were first tested with several supervisors to ensure they elicited deep and focused responses. We asked all participating supervisors:

1. *What is the single, most important piece of advice PhD students need to heed to thrive in their doctoral program?*
2. *PhD students often hear, "you should do this … or that," but what behavior or thought patterns do you think are most important for PhD students to avoid?*

Asking for brevity created the conditions for these outstanding supervisors to hone in on what they felt was most important to share with PhD students for their success and to communicate it effectively.

Responses were received from seventy-four scholars across eight countries and myriad disciplines. The scholars' expertise spans fields as diverse as Chemistry, Communication, Economics, Education, Environmental Law, Epidemiology, Medicine, Neuroscience, Political Science, Russian Literature, and many more. This broad spectrum ensures that the advice collected is enriched by diverse academic traditions and cultural contexts, offering PhD students varied and valuable insights to better navigate their doctoral journeys.

Limits of the Advice

It is important to note that while broad and diverse, the advice we collected does not comprehensively represent supervisors globally or culturally. While all efforts were made to obtain full disciplinary and regional representation, the responses we received dictate the geographic and disciplinary diversity presented. In other words, we did not leave anyone out in our invitations but had little control over who responded. While our respondents are representative of diverse cultures, aspects of cultural influence, positionality, and unique challenges faced by some students – such as those with differing abilities or who are neurodivergent – may not feature prominently in their advice. At the end of this publication, we have included brief bios that describe the professional backgrounds and experiences of each contributor to support readers in understanding the range of perspectives included.

The full range of cultures throughout the world that influence graduate studies is not represented in our collection of advice. Also, the strength of the book – the questions that asked supervisors for their best advice about what to do and what not to do – emphasizes general aspects of graduate student mindset, processes, and habits that apply broadly, even beyond the graduate program. With these questions, some aspects of the work and the graduate studies environment are not prominent. In fact, the responses in their entirety relate to what the graduate can do or not do: their agency. Hence, not all specific challenges facing PhD students are well addressed, such as how to acclimatize in international contexts or prepare for examinations.

The advice presented is not comprehensive. It is all excellent advice from excellent supervisors, but we recognize that there are other perspectives on what leads to success in

PhD studies, including those from minoritized supervisors, supervisors with differing abilities, and supervisors with experience supporting diverse needs. We encourage you not to stop here with your skill and personal development but rather continue to seek additional advice and resources for growth and to address specific issues beyond the scope of this work. We have included a list of further reading at the end of the book to get you started.

And finally, remember that the advice from each of the supervisors who contributed to this book with the goal of helping you was limited to two questions. The advice they've given does not represent the whole of their opinions or thoughts on the matter, nor a comprehensive guide to all aspects of a graduate program. Instead, the small pieces of each supervisor's guidance collectively create a kaleidoscope of wisdom about what actions are most important for graduate students to take and not take during the course of their studies.

About the Authors

We, the authors and editors of this book, are educators with over forty years of combined experience developing effective learning activities.

Dr. Judy Wearing has specialized experience in designing activities to support critical thinking and other competencies. Judy is a Lead Learning Architect and author. She has two PhDs, one in experimental biology from the University of Oxford, the other in creativity in education from Queen's University.

Dr. Christopher DeLuca is a professor of education, a curriculum and assessment specialist, and former Associate Dean at the School of Graduate Studies and Postdoctoral Affairs, Queen's University. He has published over 140 articles and book chapters and has worked extensively with graduate students as a supervisor, committee member, and examiner.

Dr. Stephen MacGregor is an assistant professor of educational leadership, policy, and governance at the University of Calgary's Werklund School of Education. He is also a recent PhD graduate and has been instrumental in "testing" the advice for its value to the lived experiences of PhD students. He continues to support graduate students directly through his supervision but also as the representative to the New Scholar Advisory Board for the Canadian Educational Researchers' Association and a network coordinator for the International Congress for School Effectiveness and Improvement.

Getting Started: Toward a More Prosperous PhD

We elected to frame this book around the notion of prosperity because its etymology resides in "hope" and "success." The term *prosperous* derives from old Latin, *pro* ("for") plus *spes* ("hope"), and later from Latin *prosperō* ("I cause to succeed"). It is our hope that the advice and strategies in this book empower you to succeed in your PhD. Whether you are just considering a PhD or have nearly completed one, this book will help you move forward successfully with your goals. Many pieces of advice throughout this book call on you to reflect on why you are pursuing a PhD and encourage you to be your authentic self along the doctoral journey. Of course, this means that some will realize that the PhD journey is not one they wish to take. Being your authentic self might mean pursuing goals outside the hallowed halls of the academy and contributing to society in other ways. In fact, the skills and knowledge gained during a doctoral program – whether you are in a PhD program for one year or ABD – are highly transferable and can lead to fulfilling careers in a variety of fields. Research has shown that many graduate students find fulfillment in careers beyond academia,[19,20,21] applying their skills in industry, government, and non-profit sectors where their ability to conduct rigorous research, analyze complex data, and think critically is highly valued. We encourage you to explore and be open to diverse careers, recognizing that a fulfilling and impactful PhD can lead you down myriad paths.

You can read this book from cover to cover or select chapters that are most relevant or timely for you. The advice in each chapter is framed by a summary narrative that positions the chapter theme in relation to the doctoral journey. Each chapter concludes with reflection and application activities that ask you to translate the advice to your specific doctoral practice. Remember, this book is intended to support you and your specific PhD. Your job is to consider the advice in relation to your experience. Some pieces of advice will resonate more than others. Use the activities at the end of each chapter to make meaning from the themes and advice, and to establish concrete plans for greater success in your PhD. We now invite you to dive in and start down the path of a more prosperous PhD.

CHAPTER TWO

Make Wise Choices

Countless choices punctuate PhD programs. Among the most significant, a PhD student must choose an appropriate supervisor; a higher education institution; research interests and a specific research topic; research collaborations to embark on; and what, when, and where to publish. The universe of possible choices expands even further when considering those of a more personal nature, such as living arrangements that may last but a few years. Naturally, making well-informed decisions – that may be described as *wise* – is central to a positive and successful doctoral experience. But how do we go about ensuring our decisions are "wise"? We had better clear up this question if you are to find the advice in this book useful! A key realization is that simply identifying the major challenges of doctoral education is not sufficient to ensure success. Instead, we must openly examine *how* we arrive at specific choices, particularly the messiness of incorporating evidence such as external advice and lessons learned from past experiences.

It is tempting to envision our decision-making process flowing neatly from evidence to decisions. Yet, we know from the work of scholars like Daniel Kahneman[1] that linear pathways from evidence to thinking to action are an over-simplification. A complex blend of assumptions, relations, and contextual factors influences how we make decisions. What's more, "without conscious deliberation [...] decisions often take shape gradually [...] through small uncoordinated steps."[2] Making efforts to understand this process helps you recognize and navigate the inherent complexities in making decisions during your PhD. How, then, can you conceptualize the decision-making process for the many choices you encounter? Tim Cain and colleagues[3] have developed a practical model to do just that. We represent their model as follows:

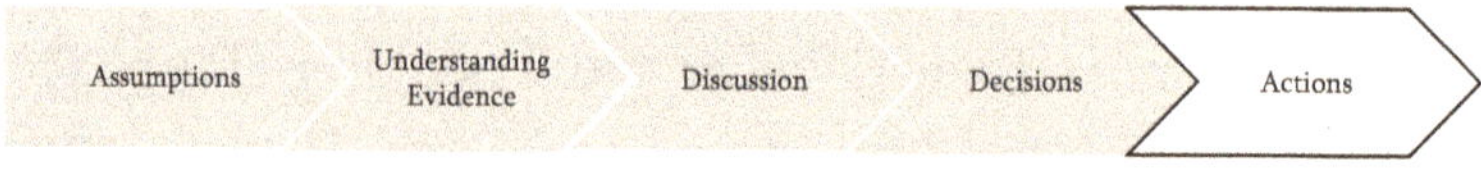

You can use this model, combined with the advice from leading supervisors featured below, to draw out important lessons for the choices you encounter in doctoral programs. These lessons empower your ability to make wise choices.

Get to Know Your Assumptions

It is crucial to examine how our personal histories (i.e., prior intentions, relations, and experiences)[4] give rise to our spoken and unspoken **assumptions** about research and higher education. We offer two key lessons for PhD students that flow from this discussion:

1. Be *attentive* to your assumptions as they are called upon to inform a decision.
2. Be *intentional* about analyzing the veracity of your assumptions and how they serve you.

To illustrate the importance of examining your assumptions, take for instance the assumptions generally held about institutional research performance metrics as an indicator of a potential positive doctoral student experience. The reasoning is plain to follow: a university that produces internationally renowned research is likely home to many leading researchers as well as research support services and facilities; hence, one might expect similar quality in the research training opportunities. However, studies of the doctoral student experience reveal that such links are not so clear-cut.[5] One issue is that institutional rankings and metrics are notoriously easy to manipulate. As the popular author and staff writer at *The New Yorker* Malcolm Gladwell put it, "it's an act of real audacity when a ranking system tries to be comprehensive and heterogeneous."[6] In other words, any simple ranking of something as complex as "research performance" is not likely to tell you much about an institution, especially the experience it provides for PhD students, let alone *your* PhD experience. Much more important are qualities such as the learning environment, opportunities for comprehensive scholarly development (research, teaching, and service), and social connections among faculty, staff, and students.

In another example, it is common to hear fledgling PhD students talk as if academia is the assumed career trajectory following a doctoral program. At the same time, you have likely heard that career prospects for aspiring academics are uncertain in the best of circumstances, depending on your discipline, willingness to relocate, and scholarly productivity and impact. Now, imagine the feeling of drifting toward an academic career for which you have a tepid interest, passively accepting this path as the "correct choice." It is easy to see how you could end up discouraged by the experience and job prospects, not to mention dubious about the value of a PhD in the first place. However, even a cursory analysis of this assumption reveals its failings. Many professionals pursue doctoral degrees, and the vast majority go on to find fulfilling careers inside and outside of academia. The reality is that pursuing a doctorate can serve other, equally valid motives for becoming an academic, including general career development, personal growth, or contributing to social justice. To fully appreciate these opportunities, you only need to question your assumptions about what a PhD graduate *should* do.

While these are only two illustrative examples, they represent the pitfalls of letting assumptions go unexamined and of using proxy measures of performance metrics in lieu of a critical examination of the advantages and disadvantages that really matter to you. Doing so restricts your ability to make an informed decision. The consequences may be dire.

Weigh the Evidence

With assumptions analyzed, we must next acknowledge that any **evidence** we use to make wise choices cannot speak for itself; it requires interpretation. Evidence is always in the making, context-dependent, and moderated by what we already know.[7] As a result, every choice requires that you weigh and compare the available evidence and determine its limits and trustworthiness. Once you establish whether additional evidence is needed, you need to determine how to go about collecting and analyzing it. What does this mean for a PhD student bearing down on decisions about their program of study?

First, consider your *why* for pursuing a doctoral degree. Curiosity is surely part of the mix, but we wager there are also societal motivations – something that irked you enough about the status quo that made you ask, "How can I make things better?" This societal motivation should directly inform the way you gather and interpret evidence, recognizing that your research has broader societal implications. Regardless of the primary beneficiaries of your research (e.g., practitioners, policymakers, community members), their perspectives can enrich the research process in ways that are unavailable if you silo-up and treat research as a purely academic endeavor. Let's take the example of equity research in education. As an emerging scholar looking to speak the language of your field, you might feel inclined to give primacy to classic scholarly texts that discuss the experiences of marginalized student populations. However, incorporating the lived experiences of teachers, school administrators, students, or parents through collaboration can enrich and potentially challenge the academic narratives. Many studies of collaborative research suggest this is possible.[8] But how should you integrate academic and non-academic evidence, or perhaps more challenging, how should you balance your perspective with that of other research partners? There are no simple answers. It is ultimately up to you to decide how diverse perspectives and experiences will preferentially inform your research and wider doctoral journey.

As a second example, consider the selection of a supervisor. The choice tends to involve a combination of factors such as the individual's reputation, your intellectual compatibility, and other pragmatic benefits like funding and a positive working environment.[9] You might also be concerned with more personal relationship factors, such as whether you will develop a personal connection. The decision is complicated, even within this artificially narrowed universe of factors that deserve attention. Simply put, many of the most important choices lack ideal options and involve trade-offs. To make a wise decision, you must accept that selecting a supervisor will first require you to weigh the factors of greatest personal importance. Connecting these examples back to the topic of evidence, we can distill three more lessons about making wise decisions:

1. Evidence comes in many forms, and you must determine how to preferentially weigh it.
2. Evidence is never complete, meaning you must consistently update your understanding of it and recognize where it falls short.
3. Evidence cannot, in itself, tell you how to act.

Seek Advice, Wisely

The third element in decision-making is **discussion**, gathering the thoughts and perspectives of trusted others. As the following chapter, Foster Relationships, discusses in much greater detail, pursuing a PhD is not meant to be a solitary experience. However, when it comes to making wise choices, the best course of action is not as simple as "seek out help." Studies of the supervisor-student relationship find that autonomy and perceived competence are both foundational building blocks for success in a doctoral program.[10,11,12] When a supervisory relationship is too distant, PhD students may become overwhelmed by the volume of choices they face – their competence is at risk; conversely, when the relationship is too directive or involves intense governance, the same students may struggle to develop their identity as independent researchers – their autonomy is at risk. Although your supervisor or committee will almost certainly be willing to offer advice on a variety of questions or concerns about your research, program, or professional trajectory, they cannot provide the *right* choice for a given decision. In fact, the advice offered by your supervisor or advisors may, at times, misalign with your interests or circumstances. The same is true for all personal and professional interactions involving the sharing of advice. From this duality of both appreciating the importance of social discussions and maintaining autonomy, we reach the final lessons of this chapter:

1. Seek advice widely but recognize that advice is shared from the advice giver's own personal vantage point.

2. Respect your autonomy while welcoming support during times of heightened turbulence and uncertainty.

The advice featured in this chapter brings the lessons discussed above to life. Whether focused on analyzing assumptions, understanding evidence, or having discussions, each scholar provides a way of thinking about the doctoral experience that enriches your ability to make wise choices. At the same time, despite everything presented in this chapter, perhaps the most important takeaway is that you should expect to get it wrong sometimes. This, too, is part of learning to make wise choices.

ADVICE ON MAKING WISE CHOICES

Befriend and respect your questions. First, your big question – the wonderment or problem that has hold of you and won't release its grip. The question to which you return gladly each day, even when facing it feels like dealing with a cranky two-year-old. Then, the questions that arise from your reading, coursework, conversations, and the ones that seem to pop up out of nowhere. Keep a journal of your questions. Write them down. Ponder their dimensions, approaching them with a gentle, non-grasping attention, with playful curiosity. Sketch out the threads of relationship among your questions. Take them for a beer or for tea. Let them delight you. And, when they seem to be taking you in multiple, even contradictory, directions, love them even more. Pause, breathe deeply, and you might glimpse a hint of the contours of a deeper issue, or underlying coherence that animates your work.

Why honor your questions? They are your lifeline, your gyroscope, your pivot point in the process of graduate study. Lifeline – questions are the best clues to the arc of your intellectual narrative, the distinctive insights you carry that constitute your contribution to a field. Gyroscope – questions stabilize, allowing more discriminating judgments about possible lines of argumentation or bodies of material that invite engagement. Pivot point – your questions are the place from which you connect your project to larger conversations, past and present. Questions situate you alongside rather than above or beneath others in your field. Questions shine the light toward insights you carry but for which you do not yet have language.

Imagine your questions as the semi-permeable membrane of a living cell. They provide the edges or boundaries for an emerging project and they are the conduit through which it receives nourishment from the vast sea of data, texts, and insights of other scholars. Befriend and respect your questions. Honor them and let them help you – to create, to contribute, to experience delight, and to avoid losing yourself.

Patricia O'Connell Killen,
Pacific Lutheran University, Religion

Learn how to ask a good question. Doctoral programs are very good at teaching the tools of research, including how to design a study, how to collect and analyze data, how to write up an article, how to navigate the publication process.

They are also good at teaching the prior art: what smart people used to write about, what eminent theorists used to theorize about, and (in a typical doctoral seminar) why they all got it wrong in ways large and small. But they are not as good at pointing out the kinds of problems that the world needs solved, which is the essence of a good question today. Society is facing enormous, often existential threats, from the declining health of democracies to increasingly intrusive surveillance by corporations and governments to global pandemics to the climate emergency. What the world needs most from smart people is forward-looking thinking to take on these challenges.

Academia is the only institution in society with a critical mass of motivated smart people with the breadth and depth of knowledge to take on these challenges. But we are not great at training young scholars to ask the right questions. The monastic life of the graduate student, and the pressure to publish early and often (on whatever topic the journals favor), undermines the effort to identify the right kinds of questions. Rather than asking "Where is a gap in the literature that I can fill?," ask "What is a problem worth addressing that my field and my skills are uniquely suited to take on?" Keep reading the news. Keep engaged with the world. Find the places where what you know how to do and what the world needs to have done fit together. You will be happier in your work, and your family will be proud of what you do.

Jerry Davis,
University of Michigan,
Management and Organizations

Most doctoral students require considerable support with the process of writing a dissertation because it is extremely challenging. Consequently, in order to thrive in a doctoral program, it is extremely important that students choose a supervisor who shares their interests, works collaboratively, and makes it a priority to be accessible and provide feedback. Supervisors typically interview potential doctoral students and choose students who, in addition to outstanding academic qualifications, share their interests. Students should also interview supervisors to ensure compatibility of interests and style. For example: some students prefer to work individually and others in a team. Therefore, when choosing a supervisor, ask about whether they facilitate teamwork or prefer independence.

Judy Wiener,
University of Toronto,
Psychology and Human Development

Work out why your PhD is important. You are going to be working on these questions for at least three years and possibly the rest of your working life so choose a topic that matters. Curiosity is enough for some but the most fulfilling work is that which can improve the world around you. Challenge yourself to think about how your findings can make a difference – What decisions will your work inform? Who needs to make those decisions? What difference will it make if they listen to your findings? This will help you ask the right questions and stay motivated to overcome the many obstacles you will face. Make sure that your findings are accessible and relevant to those who can use them to make a difference, not just your supervisors, examiners, and other academics.

Andrew Hayward,
University College London,
Epidemiology and Public Health

Find a question or topic that excites your curiosity and whose exploration gets you going in the morning and possibly keeps you up at night. Faculty and colleagues will readily offer advice, most of it well meaning, on what should be your research focus. Weigh their advice carefully but at the end of the process your research, as exemplified by but not limited to your dissertation, must be the questions and methods that excite you the most and with which you most want to be identified. Don't let guesses about what are the "hot" topics or what research is most likely to get you a job at the end of the process guide your decisions. First, projects chosen on that basis are unlikely to provide the sustained motivation required to push through the frustrations and long hours associated with any research project and that are required to complete a successful dissertation. Secondly, the hot topic today is unlikely to be the hot topic several years from now when you enter the job market. How does one find the right topic? The best ways are through exploration via seminar papers early in your graduate education and work as a research assistant for different faculty members. Use seminar papers as a way to explore a topic with an eye to whether it could evolve into a dissertation. RA work is a key component to the search process. It introduces you to the current topics and methods in a subfield and is by far the best and maybe only way to learn how to do research. One does not acquire the skills to begin and complete a research project by reading the journals. This is, after all, still a craft profession and supervised learning is the best way to learn the craft. Okay, I have slipped in two pieces of advice, but they are really aspects of one piece.

John Jackson,
University of Michigan, Political Science

We sometimes treat doctoral theses like they should be a definitive and groundbreaking contribution; not so. That's the kind of work we should expect from scholars in the later years of their career. Instead, think of your doctoral work as the opportunity to advance the conversation in an area that you care about. Your insights do not need to be definitive, earthshaking, or the "final word." They do need to be novel. But remember, for most graduate work you are joining a conversation that long precedes you. Write something you care about; something important. But relieve yourself of the stress of seeking a contribution that would win you a Nobel Prize.

Kim Brooks,
Dalhousie University, Law

One piece of advice I would give any PhD student is to have an idea of the thesis topic as early as possible so that research and coursework can be coordinated in select areas right from the start. For example, my thesis director told me, after six years of work, that he thought I should read the silver age Latin poets and add a chapter on them. That would have added another two years to my thesis work … get my Latin up to literary levels, read all the silver age poets and poems, compare them with my poet and poems for sources and imitation ... it was, in my opinion, a total waste of time. Luckily, I had discussed that particular area with José Manuel Blecua in Barcelona, Spain (the top Quevedo specialist worldwide). He told me to stay clear of classical sources and to analyze "what the poet actually wrote" in the light of the works of his contemporaries. I explained this to my thesis director, and he backed off. "Well, if Blecua said that, I guess we can forget my idea."

Now, if I'd wanted to do what my thesis director suddenly wanted, I would have needed to have taken up Latin (again) much earlier, and I would have needed to double up on a series of courses that gave me the Latin/Spanish background. This would have changed the direction of my thesis, but it would have added years to my completion time.

My advice is: think broadly, plan from the start, and try to hone in with your coursework and research on the specific areas that you want to specialize in. Write course projects and essays that line up with your research area so that you can use them as preliminary research and then rewrite them and/or incorporate them later. Above all, keep your eyes open. Doctoral work is a wonderful journey during which you will grow and develop: enjoy that journey and don't worry too much about the destination.

Roger Moore,
St. Thomas University,
Spanish Language and Literature

Do not be afraid of really hard work and long hours. The best PhD students will not shy away from collaboration opportunities, rather they will seek them out. These opportunities are many – faculty with unfinished projects, fellow students extending a class idea, responses to recently published papers. There will be many of these that come across your desk. Now is the time to say "Yes." Don't worry about being overcommitted (besides, all successful faculty are overcommitted!). Similarly, you should not avoid a project because you think you don't have the skills (yet) to do it. Rather, learn the skills. So, if you don't know a programming language necessary to do the project, learn the language. If you are not familiar with the dataset that's being proposed, learn the dataset. If you don't know a literature, learn the literature. The mantra should not be "I can't do that ..."; it should be "I haven't failed yet."

Generally, academic success depends on early success, so you have to use the time in your PhD to build a bank of projects and prime the pipeline to have a continuous stream of work come out. This will mean that you have to put in very long hours – I know of no successful academic that's working a forty-hour week. Particularly when you are young and getting started, expect much more. At least in most research-oriented American academic departments, graduate students are funded to complete the PhD. Always remember that this is a remarkable opportunity that represents a real investment of funds and resources that could have gone to something or somebody else, and there is probably somebody out there who is hungrier, more eager, or simply willing to work harder. So treat the time at your PhD as having won the "golden ticket" – and avail yourself of every opportunity that you can.

James Moody,
Duke University, Sociology

PhD students need to be extra careful in choosing their dissertation advisor because their completion is predicated on how well they communicate with their advisors. All too often, students choose based on areas of interest without taking personal interaction style into account. Otherwise, they end up with a great name who is not very good interpersonally and who has set ideas about how to write a dissertation rather than working out what works best for a particular student.

Fatma Müge Göçek,
University of Michigan, Sociology and Women's Studies

There are so many necessary conditions for success that it is difficult to single one out. Being limited to one, I would identify the importance of maintaining enthusiasm in one's research. There are many doctoral students who lose interest or heart, and merely drag themselves over the finish line, or quit en route. While some loss of enthusiasm is driven by external events (people fall in love or receive, unsolicited, unimaginably exciting and lucrative job offers), my sense is that most of it is driven by uninspired selections of dissertation topics. The path of least resistance when it comes time to a dissertation is to make a modest extension of existing work or of an advisor's project. Avoid this, unless you have convinced yourself that your work will be a significant step forward, and that it is worth two to four years of your life – and, ideally, will propel a research trajectory for several years beyond that.

Charles Becker,
Duke University, Economics

Although I wish it wasn't true, if your goal is to become a professor, then your ability to land a faculty position will depend primarily on the quality and quantity of the research you are able to publish as a graduate student. Due to this, my advice to you is to be selfish during your years as a graduate student. By "selfish" I mean don't spend time doing research that someone else is more excited by than you are but, rather, make totally sure you love the topic you are researching. If you love it, if you deeply want to gain a better understanding of it, and especially if you see the value in gaining such an understanding ... then the research is easy because it's fun and intrinsically interesting. So, if you're not sure about the research you are initially doing, find out what you are interested in, find out who is doing that work, and despite all the discomfort and logistics, find a way to work with that person doing what you love. The research you do in graduate school will define your expertise and may thus become the research you do for the next forty years, so choose something you want to be an expert on, something that fits who you are and what you want to learn more about.

Also realize that becoming a professor is just one pathway open to you. The skills you are learning are valued in many non-academic settings, and if your school does not yet do a good job making you aware of the other possible pathways, perhaps initiate something on your campus where you bring in nontraditional guest speakers. It's a great way to begin networking with relevant individuals and learning the variety of things you might do with your degree.

Steve Joordens,
University of Toronto, Psychology

Don't fake it. Make it. Thriving in a doctoral program means arriving at your commencement ceremony, which means you completed and defended your dissertation. The dissertation you wanted to research, write, and edit because you had something to say, something to contribute to the academic field you chose. Your dissertation that consumed years of your life until you bought that Phinally Done coffee mug. You made it. What I've just thumbnailed may seem a predetermined path and inevitable outcome for PhD students. Why would one do otherwise? As a longtime dissertation director and recent graduate program administrator (as well as a former graduate student), I've found that PhD students sometimes pitch projects they think potential directors want to hear rather than the projects they really want to pursue. Why does faking it happen, and how can you take the path of making it instead?

Approaching a professor about directing your dissertation can be daunting. If you did your MA elsewhere as I did, you may not have had much time to meet many of your new faculty and get a sense of their mentoring style. The professor you targeted in your application may have been on leave when you were doing coursework. You may have done your best seminar paper for a professor whose primary research interests intersect with yours but aren't quite the same. (Tip: That's a good move.) Or the research aims and desired dissertation director you put on your application may have changed. (Tip: Applications are not contracts; it's fairly common to shift research interests during coursework.) Factor in limited years of funding and that's considerable pressure before a doctoral student has secured a director. So sometimes doctoral students will pitch a dissertation they assume will get them to Yes. But when PhD students fake interest in a project, they are less likely to complete degrees on time – and to publish their research later as a book or journal articles.

In the book disciplines, graduate students do their dissertation research and writing individually, proposing projects on their own. Yet PhD students who work in teams can also see themselves as makers of their dissertations, as the genesis of the lengthy document they deposit in their university libraries – documents that bear their names. To make is to bring into existence something you frame, form, and fashion. Being the composer of your dissertation (or portion of one) makes you more likely to commit to its completion because it first and foremost generates from you. And you continue working on it and responding to your mentor's feedback because you're fully invested. You made it.

Marsha Bryant,
University of Florida, English

To thrive in their doctoral programs, PhD students should carefully choose and foster strong working relationships with their supervisors and, when making choices about research topics, follow their passion. It is challenging for students to thrive if they are at odds with their supervisors. Supervisors provide guidance, expertise, resources, access to networks, and so forth. They influence students' progress in subtle and overt ways and significantly shape student competencies and experience. This said, students' experiences are also shaped by their interest in their work.

Students may have limited options related to the courses they take, but students' research has the potential to be shaped by their areas of curiosity and passion. PhD students will spend months and often years immersed in doctoral thesis research. If they do not find it intrinsically rewarding to explore thesis research areas, the long doctoral journey can seem endless. If students are highly motivated to study issues related to their thesis, the hard work and perseverance involved in the thesis research are more likely to seem well worth it. The student is more likely to enjoy and complete the thesis research and PhD degree requirements.

Yolande E. Chan,
McGill University, Digital Technology

Rather than focusing solely on the end goal, the true value of a PhD lies in the process. For most people, at the end of the day a PhD certifies your ability to conduct and think about research; it doesn't require you to emerge as the foremost expert in your field (although that would obviously be nice). High levels of recognition usually follow years of diligent work after the PhD.

Undertaking a PhD may be the only time in your life when you have the freedom and resources to explore topics deeply, learn and master new skills, venture into tangential areas, and then return enriched with broader and more meaningful insights. This time is a privilege – use it. While you might feel pressed for time now and hesitant to add in extra challenges, future workplace commitments will probably offer fewer opportunities for such immersive engagement and time for learning.

Each skill you learn during a PhD is a strategic investment, even if doesn't feel like it at the time. The specific demands of future jobs are unpredictable and while you might have a career path in mind when you start the PhD, the future job market is uncertain, and the types of skills needed are constantly evolving. Your interest, and your personal situation and responsibilities (especially with respect to family and relationships), may also change over the course of a PhD, so having a diverse set of skills and experiences in your toolkit to draw upon and position yourself with at the end can provide a crucial advantage and open doors to unexpected career paths once you've completed.

Elizabeth R. Peterson,
University of Auckland, Psychology

I write from the perspective of an experimental scientist, specifically a chemist interested in non-carbon-based energy conversion and storage, and catalysis in chemical reactions. However, my doctoral studies and subsequent career did not start with these foci, so I hope to offer here some thoughts that students might consider in moving forward on such a journey. Getting a PhD involves a long time commitment (an average of four to five years) with a major component of original research that produces periods of frustration and moments of exhilaration. It is not for everyone but for those who complete the journey, it is a time of fulfillment and joy.

So where to start? What are key factors and considerations you should have at the outset of your doctoral program, aside from courses and requirements that must be taken or fulfilled? The key component is actual hands-on research. As such, the PhD program is for one who has a persistence to explore, a drive to learn, and in experimental science, the willingness to assess (and reassess) the research. This may include analysis of what you have accomplished research-wise to date, and if necessary, the drive to redefine and reroute the scientific project on which you have embarked.

The most important choices at the outset of the program are what to study project-wise and with whom. Personally, I think the choice of thesis advisor is most critical because the relationship between student and PhD mentor is potentially one of the most rewarding in life. That certainly was the case for me when I began graduate study at Columbia University and chose to work with an inspiring junior faculty member (our relationship is now over fifty years old and remains a delight for both of us). However, no matter the age of the advisor, student-mentor communication is central to the research and the appreciation you will develop for your research. It is not (and never should be) a matter of getting marching orders from the advisor with respect to what is to be done next. Here is where real collaboration develops – an analysis of what has been done and the next steps forward in moving the project along. Discussion with lots of "if-then" scenarios.

In most research labs, there are, in addition to the PhD mentor, others who are also conducting research, ranging from postdoctoral and advanced graduate students to others like yourself, as well as undergraduate research students. Collaboration in such an environment is both essential and deeply meaningful. You do research, you learn, and you teach, with fractions of each changing as you work toward your thesis and progress through graduate school.

Most importantly, you, the student, are key to how well the research progresses. You discover and analyze, and with your advisor and research group colleagues, you assess, reassess, and move forward. When success is achieved, you will get a sense of fulfillment and achievement that no other academic endeavor can provide. In this context, graduate school will be one of your life's highlights, and I wish you success in it.

Rich Eisenberg,
University of Rochester, Chemistry

I would advise the student to find a relevant problem for research that they can fall in love with. Passion is an important factor in research, but passion guided by reason and equanimity. Such a research problem can be found either through reading research papers, or through research seminars or from advanced graduate courses.

Ram Murty,
Queen's University, Mathematics

My advice would be to "get out more" – to avoid getting stuck in an academic rut, dominated by a single disciplinary perspective or intellectual paradigm. As a student studying Geography, I strayed into Anthropology and Cultural Studies, which enriched my world view and introduced me to new ways of thinking. It gave my dissertation a more ethnographic dimension, challenging the predominantly quantitative way of thinking that was common at the time. Reading Stuart Hall, Raymond Williams, and bell hooks started as a personal interest but gradually showed me an alternative way of framing the field of social and cultural geography. These days, I work with bioscientists and health researchers, sociologists and historians – all committed to food system transformation, where working across disciplinary boundaries is so much more productive and enriching than working in academic silos. Starting out on this journey at graduate school set the tone for a career of crossing boundaries and challenging conventions – a path I'd encourage others to follow.

Peter Jackson,
University of Sheffield, Human Geography

I think the essential thing for PhD students is to choose (in consultation with their supervisors of course) a topic they are passionate about. The PhD has to be sustainable for three to four years or more and if the student is not passionate and driven to explore their research question in all its beautiful, frustrating, and wonderful intricacies, it may begin to feel overwhelming, drawn out, and potentially unsustainable. I have seen students plug away for years on awful topics that they didn't choose, didn't like, and didn't feel passionate toward and they often end up quitting or simply hating their topic and even their thesis. This seems like a travesty and very avoidable if the right (for them) topic is chosen.

Margaret Simmons,
Monash University, Medicine

REFLECTION AND APPLICATION ACTIVITIES

In the PhD forums on social media, one of the most common questions goes something like this: "What's a good research topic in [global economics/gender studies/astrophysics ... insert your topic here]." One of the most common responses to this question goes something like this: "Read the literature, find a gap, and there's your topic." This basic exchange removes the notion that the human who's doing the research has a personal history, personal interests, and personal talents and abilities – all of which have tremendous influence on PhD students' success.

The advice in this chapter that emphasizes choice of topic suggests choosing a novel, important topic that you are passionate about. But how do you do this? The activity Deep Diving into Your "Why" is designed to help you get at what you find purposeful and important. The advice in this chapter also focuses on the importance of your choice of supervisor, with many factors mentioned. The Prosperous PhD Decision-Making Tool takes you step by step through your own decision-making process to make the choices that will work best for you. How Much Do I Love My Project helps you assess the degree of passion you hold for your chosen topic.

Activity 1: Deep Diving into Your "Why"

Ask yourself the question: *Why am I doing a PhD in [insert research field]?* The initial response from many PhD students invariably emphasizes practical life concerns: jobs, family, money. Some people are in touch with additional emotional motivations, such as status, or making their parents proud. By repeatedly asking "why," "why," "why," however, deeper motivations come to light, and you get to the root of why you are *really* doing your PhD. Figuring this out helps build motivation and clarifies future actions. To show how this activity works, here is an unrelated example:

> The querent asks, *why am I interested in starting an investment account?*
> Their first response: *To gain wealth.*
> Their second *why* question – *why does wealth matter?*
> Their response: *So I can retire earlier.*
> Their third *why* question – *why do I want to retire early?*
> Their response: *Because I want freedom from the pressure of working 9–5.*
> Their fourth *why* question – *why do I feel pressure now working 9–5?*
> Their response: *Because I'm unsatisfied with my current employment and feel like it doesn't motivate me.*

By diving into the *why* of investing, we learn that the person is actually unhappy with their current job and looking for deeper motivation in their daily life. Importantly, for this activity to work, you need to repeat your answer to one "why" in the next "why."

Try it yourself. Write quickly and honestly. Make personal connections, historical connections, social connections. Explore the various "whys" that drive your research and why you are pursuing a PhD. Finding your passion, and focusing on that passion, can help you decide on what research to pursue. Then you can think of a question you are driven to answer, and/or go to the literature and find a research gap related to it.

You can use this activity multiple times, with multiple leading prompts: *Why am I doing a PhD? Why does my PhD topic matter to me?*

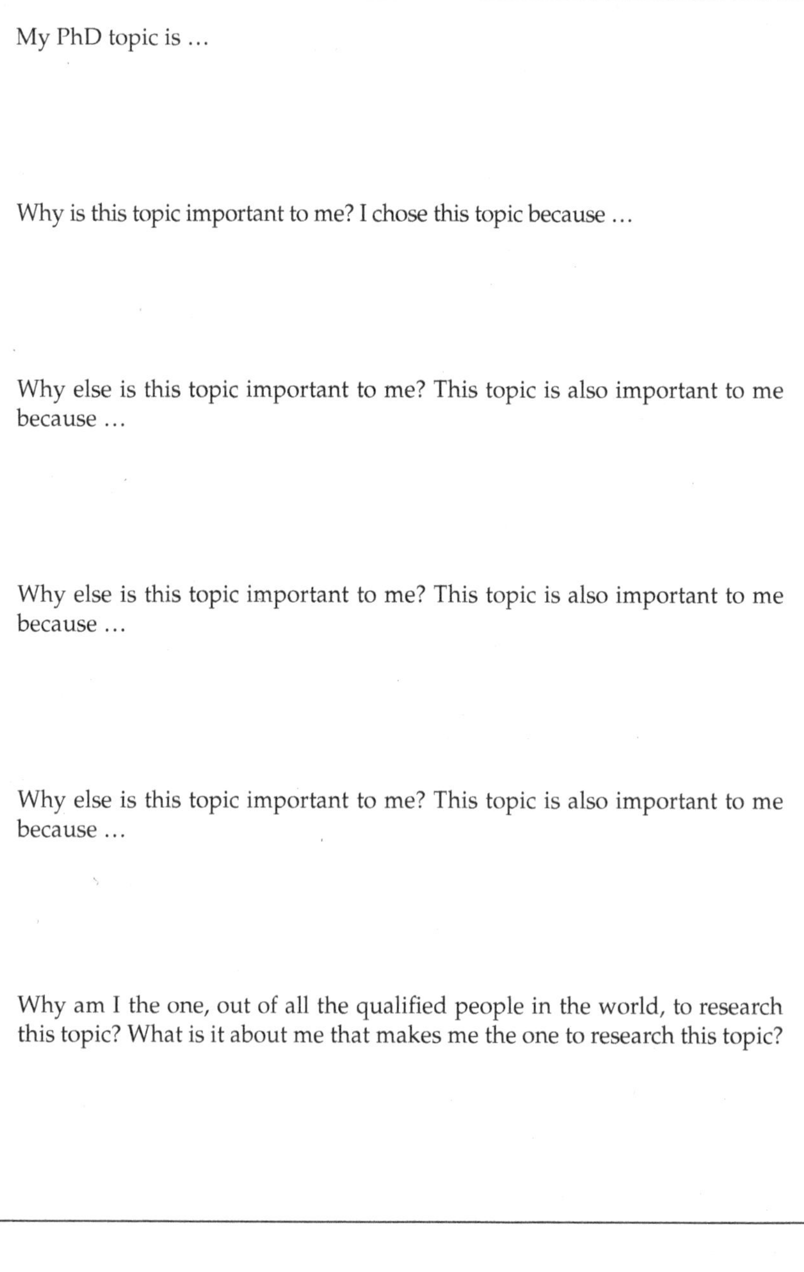

My PhD topic is …

Why is this topic important to me? I chose this topic because …

Why else is this topic important to me? This topic is also important to me because …

Why else is this topic important to me? This topic is also important to me because …

Why else is this topic important to me? This topic is also important to me because …

Why am I the one, out of all the qualified people in the world, to research this topic? What is it about me that makes me the one to research this topic?

Activity 2: The Prosperous PhD Decision-Making Tool

This tool, based on the **assumption > evidence > discuss > decide** model,[13] is designed to assist you in sorting out your thoughts with respect to two major decisions: choosing an institution and choosing a supervisor.

Institution

What factors are important to me?	Evidence I might gather	Questions I might ask	Who will I ask? Or, where will I find the information?
Location			
Reputation of my degree			
Funding for my field (research/ conferences/scholarships/ application support)			
Number and variety of faculty available			
Quality of faculty			
Research quality			
Facilities (labs/library/student wellness support, etc.)			
Equity, diversity, and inclusivity			
Other__________			
Other__________			

Supervisor

What factors are important to me?	Evidence I might gather	Questions I might ask	Who will I ask? Or, where will I find the information?
Academic reputation			
Record of graduate student support and student graduation			
Funding			
Career support for graduate students			
Social network			
Positive work relationship with students and other faculty			
Facilities			
Work style (meetings/autonomy)			
Equity, diversity, and inclusivity			
Other__________			
Other__________			

Coming to a Decision

Read over the factors above and highlight or underline two to five factors that are most important to you. Then, examine your assumptions surrounding these factors, and also the evidence you listed, as well as what questions to ask and where you'll find these answers.

Assumptions: *What assumptions am I making?*

1.

2.

3.

Discuss: *Who might I speak to about my decision? Consider a variety of relevant perspectives.*

1.

2.

3.

Gut Reaction: *What does my gut say?*

As the model in this chapter's introduction suggests, all the examining of assumptions and weighing of evidence in the world does not dictate the actual action you will take. Here are two tips to help you understand "what your gut says":

- *Flip a coin:* assign one option heads, the other tails, and flip a coin! As you do so, pay attention to your response. Did you "like" the outcome? Or did your stomach sink at the thought of having to go through with it? Or something in between?
- *Go to sleep:* delineate the question in your mind before you go to sleep. When you wake up, stay in bed for a while and let the thoughts come. In creativity theory, this is called "incubating" – letting your subconscious stew on a problem. The time between sleeping and waking is one of the best times to connect with your subconscious.

Activity 3: How Much Do I Love My Project?

The advice in this chapter emphasizes the importance of choosing a project you are passionate about. Is the curiosity and interest you feel enough to sustain you through years of research?

How curious am I towards the topic?

Mild Curiosity	1	2	3	4	5	6	7	8	9	10	Fierce Passion

How often do I find myself thinking or talking about this topic?

Never	1	2	3	4	5	6	7	8	9	10	All the Time

If I had to stop working on this research, how would I feel?

Mildly Annoyed	1	2	3	4	5	6	7	8	9	10	Devastated

If I imagine serious setbacks in this research, how motivated will I be to keep going?

Not at All	1	2	3	4	5	6	7	8	9	10	Unyielding

If I imagine writing my biography ten years from now, how proud do I feel that my PhD addressed this topic?

Not at All	1	2	3	4	5	6	7	8	9	10	Extremely

Not everyone will respond with straight tens and there are a variety of reasons for choosing to pursue a research topic. Summarize your motivation for your project and keep it close in times of challenge: *why do I love this project?*

Activity 4: The Three Rs of Reflection

Recall: I Must Remember

What are my top takeaways from this chapter?

Revise: What Do I Want to Do Differently?

Based on the advice from this chapter, what is most important for me to personally change or improve? Write down a commitment for one small action you will do differently right away.

Reimagine: What Do I Hope Will Happen?

Reimagining a future reality for ourselves and setting clear intentions is powerful in changing our current practices and achieving our goals. Based on the advice from this chapter, describe a vision of yourself in the future. A prompt for this exercise: *In one year, I hope …*

CHAPTER THREE

Foster Relationships

We recently read a tweet from a first-year teacher – someone who was beginning this new journey, which appeared as a mountain of work and challenges, much like a PhD – where she asked the world of established teacher tweeters, "What is one piece of advice you wish you had been given as a new teacher?" As we read through the over twelve hundred responses (thank goodness each tweet is capped at 280 characters!), the advice was abundantly clear: foster relationships – with colleagues, with family, with your students, with administrations, with anyone you want: just reach out and cultivate relationships! This advice parallels that from the Harvard Study of Adult Development, which tracked 268 Harvard sophomores since 1938 in the world's longest health study. The key finding was cogently summarized by lead researcher Robert Waldinger in *The Harvard Gazette* article "Good Genes Are Nice but Joy Is Better,"[1] when he stated: "The surprising finding is that our relationships and how happy we are in our relationships has a powerful influence on our health ... Taking care of your body is important, but tending to your relationships is a form of self-care too. That, I think, is the revelation."

The theme of fostering relationships is perhaps unsurprising in a book on navigating the PhD journey. We know – from countless studies and from our own experience – the importance of relationships to our health, well-being, and success. And yet, it is surprising how many PhD students believe that pursuing doctoral studies needs to be an individual, solitary, and solo activity. This belief stems, in part, from the fact that the standard for dissertation research is often articulated as *independent* and novel contributions to a field. This standard is misleading, you might even say outdated, particularly as you read journal article after journal article with author after author. It seems that, in fact, not much research is independent at all; research is inherently a collaborative act. Even single-authored works are the result of reading and relating to a field of others; engaging with, citing, and fostering relationships with scholars and colleagues that inspire thoughts, inventions, and contributions. It is foolhardy to think that our ideas and the language we use to express them are uniquely and independently our own.[2] As Bakhtin notes, "language is not a neutral medium that passes freely and easily into the private property of the speaker's intentions; it is populated – overpopulated – with the intentions of others."[3] Our work is never, singularly nor fully, our own. Instead, our scholarly work – and more importantly our ability to do scholarly work – results from our network of relationships and our openness to new ones. In that, as scholars, we should take comfort and strength.

Why are relationships so critical, not only for health but also for the PhD journey? Of the cornucopia of reasons to embrace relationships, the advice provided by scholars in this chapter points out many of them. Here we highlight six reasons – as encouragement – to take the steps necessary to reach out and forge new and deeper ground with those around you.

The first and most striking reason is that loneliness kills (Bakhtin, 1981, p. 294). Studies have pointed repeatedly to the negative health effects of living and working alone. We are social creatures who need connection to thrive – physically, emotionally, spiritually, and cognitively. Without connection to others, health deteriorates, blood pressure escalates, people die earlier, and rates of mental health illnesses rise, including depression. In relation to PhD studies, it is far too easy to cave up and write alone for days, weeks, and months on end, particularly during dissertation phases, than to engage with others to break this pattern; the pandemic has not aided this hurdle. Pulling away from this tendency toward isolation is essential for your health as well as dissertation completion.

Second, engaging with others encourages balance and healthier life choices. Many of us hate to exercise and will do anything to avoid it – even writing alone for hours until the day turns into night and the only light is the glow of the computer screen. Reaching out and committing to a workout partner can be a game changer. It's a simple interaction, but it can enable you to get out from under the screen.

Critically, the habits of work you form in graduate school become the habits you carry with you into your career; if you learn healthy work-life balance now, you set yourself in good stead for a long, healthy, and prosperous career. Key to encouraging balance and healthy life choices is recognizing that not all relationships need to be academic, deep, or lifelong. The point here is to cultivate different relationships to help engage you – your mind and body – in diverse activities that stimulate, and that bring joy, laughter, and lightness to an otherwise very heady and often sedentary existence. The result will be better academic work, guaranteed.

Third, as a budding academic, cultivating a network of relationships encourages your scholarly growth and provides inspiration for your work. Most PhD advice books would encourage the dreaded and often much-feared task of "networking" here. Instead, we offer different advice. More than one of us was asked to sit on a panel a few years ago aimed at new scholars where the topic was "how to network." We didn't know what to contribute as we didn't think of ourselves as "networkers." To us, networkers are slick pushers of their own ideas, and self-serving. Following the advice to network, one of us recounted an experience he had as a graduate student at an academic conference in which he tried to "network." He was nervous but introduced himself to one of his academic idols. He went up to her, stumbled out an introduction, complimented her on her work (as you are supposed to do), and handed her one of his papers, because he "thought she would connect with the ideas in it." She was quick to thank him and end the interaction. The whole experience was trite, brash, and awkward.

It was the first and last time he "networked," and he has since taken a different approach. Instead of networking, he just works (i.e., drops the "net" from network). When you do good work and share it in venues and spaces where the scholars you want to connect with are, then they will ask questions, conversations will happen, and relationships will be forged. The important piece here is to share your work and open yourself up to the responses and relationships of others. The outcome will be more nuanced research, unanticipated collaborations, and countless stimulating conversations to inspire your research for years.

PhDs are long journeys, three to four years on the short end and far longer for some. Life happens along the way – success, challenges, heartache, and life events. Whether related to a PhD hurdle or not, it is the people who surround us that give us perspective and encourage us to keep going. When we succeed, it is the people around us who cheer for us and champion our work. We all need motivation and motivators along the way. The fourth reason to foster relationships is to keep you motivated to finish the degree. One of us had a very difficult supervisory relationship that eventually led to switching supervisors entirely. However, it was the strong relationships with other faculty, including a trusted, independent advisor, who gave advice about the situation, as well as administration, colleagues, and friends who provided strength and support through the difficulty, that ultimately enabled perseverance. Without these relationships, the dire situation could have been much, much worse. Instead, a network of support and trust allowed for a relatively smooth transition to a new supervisor even though the initial supervisor did not take it well. At the end of the day, it was the right decision. One's mental well-being is just as important as any PhD, and such experiences are powerful in their learning value.

Fifth, as you pursue a PhD, you quickly learn that much academic work is a matter of judgment – our work is constantly being judged, refereed, and adjudicated, in formal and less formal ways. From peer-review processes to comprehensive exams to academic debates and critiques, one needs to develop a Teflon skin and separate oneself from one's work, which is far easier said than done. Our relationships can help. Our colleagues and supervisors provide a benchmark for self-reference and self-assessment. This is different than judging ourselves against others' accomplishments. From others' trajectories, we can learn about our own. Our mentors, peers, and colleagues provide reference points for our growth and development as scholars. Do I want to be like that scholar? Is my research trying to do the same thing as hers? Are my methodologies community-based and driven like … ? Our job is to engage in honest self-reflection; to understand the strengths in our work, abilities, and our inevitable opportunities for development. Having growth-oriented conversations with others about their learning journeys helps to ease the sting of judgment and establish the perspective needed to endure a degree or career of academic work.

The final reason to develop relationships throughout the PhD journey is that they present unexpected opportunities, from jobs to collaborations to lifelong colleagues, friends, and partners. The people around you help carve your life path. As cliché as it sounds, you never know who beside you in class now or who you talk to at a conference will end up offering you a job in the future or become your research partner (or better still your life partner) or your future Dean. In the end, the academic world is a remarkably small one.

This chapter centers on the importance of relationships to the PhD journey. The scholars candidly discuss the promises and pitfalls of scholarly relationships with an eye to encouraging productive supervisory, peer, mentor, and colleague relations. The advice clearly states the need to tend relationships before, during, and after pursuing a PhD – they are the stimulus and support for the journey.

ADVICE ON FOSTERING RELATIONSHIPS

The excitement of discovery, the space/time to think critically, and the opportunity to transform ideas into answerable research questions are what drive many to undertake doctoral studies. However, the emotional labor involved in completing a PhD is rarely discussed.

Embarking on the journey of a PhD is an emotionally trying experience. While you may have started the process confident in your capacities, there will be many moments along the way when doubt will seep in, and you question whether you will actually get the PhD done. Every small success seems to be preceded by a myriad of failures, and many academics will remind you that far fewer people complete a PhD than begin one. Ideas and creativity are personal, so when others bombard you with questions on the relevance, clarity, and importance of your work you might feel raw, exposed, and tempted to shut down. That is why it is important to surround yourself with people who offer encouragement to keep going, are available to provide pep talks when you doubt yourself, and who can help to normalize the emotional roller coaster involved in completing a PhD.

A writing partner is particularly valuable during the final stretches of your PhD. It can be someone to check in with regularly to share your progress (or lack thereof), set writing goals, and discuss blocks or success you are having with your writing. It can be someone willing to spend a few days with you on a retreat to a cottage or a quiet space where you spend days writing, taking breaks together to eat, go on a walk, or commiserate. It can feel surprisingly supportive to be in the same physical space with someone who is silently writing alongside you.

In many programs you will need to proactively find this level of support yourself. Doctoral programs can be great at surrounding you with resources to develop particular skills, however the Ivory Tower of objective truth is not always prepared to acknowledge the emotion behind the science. So, find PhD peers or academic mentors you can confide in and connect with on a personal level. And if possible, choose a supervisor who is willing and interested in getting to know you as a person, helping you connect your passions to your work, and sharing their own emotional journey through the PhD process. These exchanges can be as valuable as the discussions you will have on a substantive topic.

Tamara Sussman,
McGill University, Social Work

Go out of your way to make connections with faculty members at all ranks at your institution whose research interests remotely overlap with yours. Your superstar advisor might look great on your CV but might not be as up to date on research and teaching methodologies and job search strategies. You never know who might have assistantship or grant possibilities for you, or who might be on a selection committee for internal grants. In the humanities, in particular, you are well served to workshop your preliminary dissertation ideas with a wide range of scholars in multiple fields. Interdisciplinarity can give you unforeseeable advantages on the job market.

As you develop your dissertation project, explore graduate and field conferences. Seek out scholars from other institutions whose work has made an impression on you. Go to their panels and tell them of your interest. Ask questions and ask if they might consider reading a dissertation chapter for you. Expanding your network will open opportunities for you and will broaden your perspective. Then later in your dissertation-writing process these scholars might be willing to join a panel on your topic at a national field convention. In this context, you have a chance to be treated as a colleague and to find new networks within the profession.

Anne Eakin Moss,
University of Chicago, Russian Literature and Cinema

Find your people. That's harder than it sounds. By "find your people" I mean find those people who give you just the right mixture of energetic criticism and unflagging support. Either one of those offerings, to the exclusion of the other, will not take you far or be healthy to your intellectual life in the long run. Unleavened criticism erodes the vital feelings of self-worth and validation that you need over the long haul in completing a PhD degree, and undiluted praise ill equips you for the tough acts of self-criticism (and criticism from others) that our work needs to thrive and take its place in a community of thinkers.

Think of these "people" as a set of concentric circles. The center is your thesis supervisor. You may have varying degrees of choice over who that supervisor will be, but whatever your situation, use the utmost degree of choice that you can possibly have. This person will carry you through, be both your most exacting critic and heartfelt cheerleader. If that relationship isn't working and you can change it, do. If you can't change it, assemble the next concentric ring – your committee – in such a way that you can find that combination of support and critique from them. And then keep building those concentric circles: graduate student colleagues in your field; graduate colleague mentors who are in the next stages of your program; graduate colleague and/or faculty members from other colleges/universities you meet at conferences or through publication ventures who support your work; friends and family ... and just keep on building. If you're a visual thinker like me, keep a drawing of your rings of "your people" handy somewhere for those inevitable moments along the way when you feel most alone, to remind you that you're not, and remind you who to call upon.

Lorraine York,
McMaster University, Canadian Literature

Avoid letting yourself get put into a silo, both in terms of your own work and in your interactions with other graduate students. Interact with your graduate student colleagues from all subfields – listen to and learn from them and contribute to their work. Learn how to offer and accept critical comments. Your own work will be improved by this process, and you will learn to be a valued colleague.

John Jackson,
University of Michigan, Political Science

Your doctoral program involves a lengthy, intellectually intimate relationship with your supervisor(s), which you need to manage right from the very start, and perhaps even before. You can think of it as a kind of insurance, with the cheapest premium you'll ever secure or, better yet, as a mechanism to maximize the chances your doctoral experience turns out pretty close to your expectations. The premium is simply ensuring that you and your supervisor (and perhaps your advisory committee) are keenly aware of each other's interests. There are many legitimate reasons why someone might agree to supervise a PhD student, and this will influence their supervisory practice – along the continuum of "sink or swim" to "hovering micro-manager."
Discussing these with a potential supervisor will help inform your decision whether they are or are not right for you, no matter how lauded they are by the academy. Likewise, your genuine aspirations (not those you think they'd like to hear) should inform your supervisor's expectations.

A conversation that ensures a mutual understanding of the interests, motives, and expectations of both supervisor and student, preferably documented in writing, may seem like a very pessimistic way to commence a long-term relationship – a bit like prenuptial agreements anticipating a flawed union. However, it can also be a great way to build trust and mutual respect, making it much easier to have conversations when circumstances or personal growth require a change in expectations. It's also a good habit to adopt for future collaborations in any context. For example, there are some important elements of any research collaboration that absolutely require clarity, such as authorship of manuscripts that emerge from the research, and this is certainly a conversation you should have with your supervisor. Sadly, disputes over authorship are arguably the most frequent source of conflict in research collaborations and collaborating friends can quickly become professional acquaintances as a result of disputes over authorship.

Circumstances can change for both you and your supervisor, so it's a good idea to avoid surprises by checking regularly that everyone is still singing from the same songbook. A deviation might be temporary: even the most selfless supervisor will have to answer to the expectations of their institution or funding agency. More sustained or substantial deviations, or even conflicts of interest, need to be resolved rapidly. The power imbalance between supervisor and research student is intrinsic and significant. But keeping an eye on everyone's interests, through frank and documented conversations, will help ensure that other dimensions to the relationship are immensely rewarding and enduring.

Mark Elgar,
University of Melbourne, BioSciences

You need to discuss supervisory arrangements with your advisors early on in your studies and set mutually agreed ways of working. In doing this, you will ensure that you work up a collaborative arrangement rather than a boss-worker relationship. The whole aim of a PhD is to learn how to conduct independent research, and the role of the advisor is to ensure that the student does not make mistakes that can be avoided, while learning the skillset required to succeed in this endeavor. Don't choose a supervisor that hands out orders; choose one that plans a collaborative research agenda.

Tim Coulson,
University of Oxford, Zoology

Never ever criticize your PhD supervisor or research team members behind their backs. Certainly, don't play people off against each other. There is no better way to kill off all professional goodwill around you via a negative ripple effect, and the impact might well mean you are never able to build a proper career. People will label you as being troublesome, regardless of the rights and wrongs of the situation, and teams have very long memories. If you don't like your situation, it is therefore much better to negotiate a move in a positive and constructive way than carp away in the background.

Sandra Leaton Gray,
University College London, Education

In my opinion, one of the most important elements of a good PhD experience is the chemistry between the student and PhD thesis supervisor. I strongly advise the students to ascertain the possibility of establishing a good working relationship with their supervisor. Of course, there will be disagreements occasionally, but as long as the research passions and interests of the two parties are aligned, these will remain as little bumps on the road. I always viewed my PhD supervisor role as one of steering the student in the right direction in terms of developing a solid understanding of the prevailing literature and aiming at potentially fruitful research problems. Thus, the extent of the PhD supervisor's expertise in the subject matter, and their willingness to share, keeps the student away from dead ends and can save considerable time. Nevertheless, I view the chemistry with the student as primary since an experienced scholar would be able to branch out to topics which are tangential to his/her current expertise; but if the chemistry is not there that is very hard to develop through time. Therefore, my advice is to pay a lot of attention to the interpersonal relationship in choosing a supervisor.

Vedat Verter,
Queen's University, Business

You are a learner and a knower at the same time. PhD programs can be and are created to be competitive. Your fellow students are not your competition, they are your teachers. Engaging with your current and past cohorts can only strengthen your work. There is also a pattern of thinking or a desire to be independent: this is not the case. Your advisor and committee are there to guide, support, and teach you. The work sometimes gets away from PhD students because they think they "should be" doing something or have something drafted by a certain date. Also, PhD students have an idea that all of their coursework should be geared toward their dissertation – not the case. Use this time to think about your dissertation but also complementary theories, methodologies, and different ways of knowing. Do not leave your thinking about your dissertation until later in the program, this should always be in your mind – collecting information (literature) and critically thinking about your topic.

Mirna Carranza,
McMaster University, Social Work

Keep your head out of your butt (don't be a jerk) and don't become fixated by gazing at your own navel. As a future professional in whatever small community you are a part of, everyone knows everyone, and most everyone will have cleared the bar of getting a PhD. Cooperation, leadership, taking initiative, listening, planning, follow-through, and all of the things that make any community of practice function, are all part of personal character. It does not matter how clever you are if no one can stand working with you. How you fit into a social community is as critical as how you fit into an intellectual community, so do not assume that your work is self-evidently important just because you are working on it (navel-gazing), and learn how to make the case for your contribution in ways that multiple communities, including the general public or other scholarly communities, can understand and appreciate. It's your job to make that case, not theirs.

Brian P. Coppola,
University of Michigan, Chemistry

Make a list of discussion points when you have regular meetings with your supervisor and lead the conversation – nothing is more pleasant than time well used on both ends – waffle doesn't work – on either end. If you have results that you'd like to share, prepare them as a PowerPoint so you can save that, and the progress can be tangible over a time period – nothing is more frustrating for you if you have to jog your supervisor's memory every time. In that way, you have it all summarized.

Beate Kampmann,
London School of Hygiene & Tropical Medicine,
Infectious and Tropical Diseases

Avoid seeing other academics as competitors. Academia can foster a sense of competition because it is set up in such a way that people are consistently called on to identify their own expertise, contributions, or success to get ahead. Being the first author on a paper, being the lead researcher on a grant, and in some disciplines being expected to produce some work as a sole author are all ways that we give the message that individual success is the only way to get ahead. Even if you are told that it is ok to work with others, there is always an unspoken pressure to bring attention to what you yourself have done.

The truth is, to succeed in a PhD, and in academia more broadly, one needs to rely on others. The ideas developed throughout your PhD are developed collectively with the help of your supervisor and a supportive committee. Your published papers are often enhanced by integrating the input of journal reviewers who offer a different perspective and help you to push your ideas further. A fundable grant has usually been read, edited, critiqued, and encouraged by multiple people. And others tend to be most generous with their time for you when you have been generous with your time for them. So, think of other academics as allies whom you can rely on for input and who in turn can rely on you rather than as competitors whom you need to "beat," or from whom you need to hide your ideas.

Tamara Sussman,
McGill University, Social Work

When undertaking a doctoral program, start by building trusting relationships with colleagues and peers throughout your education so you do not feel alone working on your project, starting with your supervisors. Establishing trust through relationship-building is essential for a well-functioning supervision team, and as a PhD student, you play a significant role in this matter. From day one, clarify your expectations about how you want to work on your doctoral project with your supervisors and have them do the same. Being on the same page with your supervisors helps clarify the process and outcomes of your doctoral project. Striving to be open with your supervisors, not only about your doctoral project and education but also about your life outside of academia, can help promote positive psychosocial aspects of mental health, such as combating isolation, reducing anxiety and stress, and building confidence. Acknowledge that students and supervisors differ in personalities and willingness to share about their professional and personal lives, so your relationship with your supervisor might differ from that of your peers. However, your supervisors should have your back and provide support during your doctoral education. Force yourself to go to the office and get to know your supervisors and colleagues, even though it is more convenient to work from home. Seek out familiar and unfamiliar faces at social gatherings, conferences, seminars, workshops, and academic courses. The best talks happen during the coffee or lunch breaks.

Fredrik Mørk Røkenes,
University of Bergen, Education

Build a community with your peers where you not only talk about your intellectual pursuits, but you go and have fun together. Those relationships can last a lifetime and lead to all kinds of collaboration down the road. Included in the planning is the need to plan with your supervisor and committee. Talk about expectations. Learn how to take charge of your studies: set the meetings, create an agenda, take notes, follow up, and honor your deadlines. Learn about all of the tools for new researchers so you can be organized from the beginning. Be clear about what you need from your supervisory committee, and be open when you are in need of support. "Step into your academic life" and get involved in conferences, publications, and other aspects of academic life. Celebrate all of the wins along the way!

Kathryn Hibbert,
Western University, Education

Don't trap yourself in a prison of your own making. Keep your horizons broad. The more people with whom you share your work, the wider its implications will be. Don't restrict yourself to academic settings either. Consider sharing your research and interests with local schools, community centers, and non-profits. But beware of low paying adjunct teaching jobs that will eat up your time and energy. The teaching experience is not as important for the academic job market as a finished dissertation.

Anne Eakin Moss,
University of Chicago, Russian Literature and Cinema

When struggling, do not hesitate to ask for advice and support from your supervisors and peers. Don't think that your supervisors are too busy to help you. Your supervisors' job (and privilege) is to support you in your doctoral education, and they should be in your corner when you need them. It is a common misunderstanding to think that you are the only PhD student struggling with your project and are supposed to figure everything out by yourself. Steer clear of isolating yourself from your struggles for extended periods, when instead you should share them with your supervisors and peers in different forums.

Fredrik Mørk Røkenes,
University of Bergen, Education

PhD students need to avoid taking up the time of their advisor by emailing them every single idea they have; the students need to be respectful of the advisor's time, sending them material periodically, giving the advisor enough time to read and respond with feedback. Especially in writing recommendation letters, one needs ample time, at least three weeks to a month to fulfill the obligation.

Fatma Müge Göçek,
University of Michigan, Sociology and Women's Studies

Seeking Advice in a Culture of Perpetual Busyness. If you don't hear or read the words "I'm busy" from three people in your department by week's end, then your department must be an outlier. Every academic worker I know is busy-Busy-BUSY: doing research, doing service activities on campus, doing conference presentations, applying for grants and other funding, having student conferences, grading student work, teaching classes. During their initial years, graduate students take classes, too – and during their final years they apply for jobs. Yet in my experience graduate students don't tend to announce their busyness quite as much as faculty do. This divergence is surely a reason that many PhD students turn to their peers rather than their mentors for go-to professional advice.

When I supervised the graduate student teaching staff in my department, I was initially surprised at how widespread this behavior was. Then I started to think about how the academy's culture of perpetual busyness might create a reluctance to approach even the faculty member who agreed to be your mentor, your primary advisor. When mentors communicate being busy this week, PhD students may take that to mean that their mentors are always too busy to advise them. But just as teachers gotta teach, mentors gotta mentor.

Going to graduate student peers for professional advice is a good call for several things, as they have fresh takes on teaching tips, reading groups, dissertation directors, conference networking, journal submission, defense and interview preparation, even writing tips. But in many situations, there's no substitute for your mentor's advice. Consider:

1. Your peers haven't directed dissertations, and most haven't yet completed theirs;
2. Your peers don't have the vantage point to know which faculty work best together on doctoral committees;
3. With some exceptions, your peers are not journal editors; and
4. Your peers haven't read job applications.

So, when your mentor flashes the busy sign, give them a few days and approach them again. They're likely in the kind of academic crunch time we all experience every now and then. If a second email doesn't yield an appointment, drop by your mentor's office hours. Communicate why your mentor's perspective is especially valuable for the professional situation you face, and be flexible about the consultation's time and format. Consulting your mentor will usually save you time in the long run.

Marsha Bryant,
University of Florida, English

Try to avoid the assumption that your supervisor or your major professor does not need your assistance in supervising you. Supervisors and advisors cannot give their best without coaching; they can only guess how much to assist you. The most successful will give you advice only just shy of you floundering; this will give you a chance to be creative and independent but not allow you to fail. However, they may not guess right, since almost certainly they have no formal training in supervision. How might you coach your own supervisor so that your needs are met but you are not stifled? Supervisors want to exchange ideas with young scholars, but they are often reticent to engage in such trade outside their known field of expertise unless initiated by the PhD student. How might you make them comfortable so that you can reap the benefits of this exchange? Good advisors also want their students to flourish, gaining experience in written and oral communication, but again may be hesitant to appear "pushy" or "tie up" too much of your time. Do not be reticent; if you simply ignore the opportunity to coach them, then you have both missed out.

Virginia Walker,
Queen's University, Biology

You need to be comfortable with competition and be able to look after your own interests – but do not be hypercompetitive or uncooperative, do your fair share of service, and never try to make your fellow students look bad thinking it will make you look better. A supportive network of peers and mentors makes a crucial difference in your success and opens doors that right now you do not even anticipate wanting to walk through; but no one will help you if you get a reputation for treating others badly or not pulling your weight. Collaborative work can be a route to great success, and in many fields it is necessary due to the nature of the work. Be a good collaborator and a good colleague; if you're not, people find out, and they'll stop helping you.

Penny Edgell,
University of Minnesota, Sociology

Don't put up with bad behavior – on the part of faculty, peers, or undergraduates. Insist that your department or school make clear to you how you should deal with inappropriate behavior. The Director of Graduate Studies or the Chair are good resources.

Ann Waltner,
University of Minnesota, History

Do not isolate yourself. Writing a dissertation is a solitary activity but in order to be successful and healthy, a PhD should be a social experience. You therefore need a group of colleagues and collaborators, who understand what you are experiencing as a doctoral candidate and a young scholar, to reach out to when things get tough (and they will get tough). So find this crew and contribute to it. Socialize, share and be engaged with the members of your crew. This is why engaging in collaborative side projects can represent a healthy escape from your own doctoral research. Sometimes, taking a little distance from your work will give you a useful break and allow you to get back to your research with a refreshed mind. In any case, do not stay alone and isolated when doing your PhD. Reach out to others.

Thierry Giasson,
Université Laval, Journalism

Find your crew. This is coming from an introvert who does not enjoy small talk and actively avoids the kind of networking that is supposedly vital to starting and sustaining a career. Indeed, you are unlikely to find your crew by talking up the most well-connected individual or the most prominent researcher in the room. My advice is about finding connection in a work environment that, even in the "good" places, can be competitive at best and at worst, cutthroat and hostile. Where might you find your people, you ask? I cannot point a direction, but in considering my own and my colleagues' experiences, patterns appear. You are likely to find them in your own area of expertise, or at least an area close to it – too far removed, and mutual engagement may lose some of its relevance or benefit. Also, members of your crew are likely at a roughly similar career stage as you are. You are likely to share a similar set of values. And ideally you do not perceive one another as competition or adversaries. There are no rules or limits to what your crew can be about or become. They are potential coauthors who take your thinking and work in directions you would not have considered or thought possible otherwise, they are a support crew, faithful and crushingly honest proofreaders, buddies at conferences and, perhaps most importantly, a constant sounding board in a multifaceted, fast-paced work environment.

Julia N. Albrecht,
University of Otago, Business

One behavior / thought pattern to be avoided: not communicating enough, or at all, with your PhD supervisor, however busy they are, and however independent you feel you are!

Anne Petitjean,
Queen's University, Chemistry

The single most important piece of advice I can give doctoral students is for you to recognize that you are a "colleague-in-training" along the academic journey. An academic colleague-in-training provides respectful and honest help, insights, and curiosity about scholarly questions, problems, and processes. You are not simply a coworker. You are learning the skills and acquiring the experience to fully participate in the academy: learning how to review manuscripts, grants, and other scholarly works, providing thoughtful commentary that contributes to the evolution of your academic discipline, and refining big research questions. As a colleague-in-training your perspective on curriculum development and evaluation, participation in roundtables and brown-bag seminars, development of your effectiveness as a teacher, and engagement within the broader academic setting are vital to the success and survival of the university and the academic discipline. As a colleague-in-training remember that at some point in your career trajectory, you too will mentor PhD students who are beginning their process of becoming colleagues. To really thrive in your PhD program, and not merely survive, keep your focus on what is integral in shaping and promoting your development as a colleague-in-training.

Laurie Hoffman-Goetz,
University of Waterloo, Anthropology

The one thing all students need to avoid is hiding, not so much physically, although this happens, but also emotionally and intellectually. It is difficult to admit that you are struggling or that something isn't going right, especially if others around you seem to be doing well. From a supervisor's perspective, it can be frustrating when we don't see a student or hear from them for a while, or they say everything is going well, and then discover that they have been struggling for some time with a problem that we could have helped them resolve before it overwhelmed them. You may feel that you are sending out "help me" signals, but people may not be reading them as such. 1) Try to ensure that you have a couple of support people that you can go to. This may include other students, your departmental administrator, in addition to your supervisors. Your family may not necessarily understand your challenges, which can be frustrating, so finding people who are also studying or have recently completed their studies is helpful. 2) Be explicit in asking for the help that you need, when you need it. Do not suffer in silence. When you share your troubles, you will find that others have also had similar struggles. Even your supervisors are likely to have ideas from their own experiences, which you may find helpful. You won't know unless you ask.

Sarah Carr,
University of Otago, Business

REFLECTION AND APPLICATION ACTIVITIES

The advice in this chapter makes a strong argument for the importance of reaching out to others and developing strong relationships for mutual support. Who's in My Corner expands your thinking about who is available to you for potential relationships in the facets of your life that are relevant to your PhD journey. Relish these connections, take full measure of their worth, and be cognizant that relationships are mutual interactions: you are also their support.

The other activities we've included provide reflection and development of your skills in fostering relationships: they emphasize the "how" of building connections. In the Aviary provides an established tool to build trust and considers differences in personalities and preferences in all relationships, including with your supervisor. Cultural differences in communication style are relevant in our lives, and must also be considered. The Meeting Planner Template follows on the heels of advice from Marsha Bryant about "Seeking Advice in a Culture of Perpetual Busyness," clarifying expectations, and being respectful of your colleagues' time. As Virginia Walker put it, "avoid the assumption that your supervisor or your major professor does not need your assistance in supervising you."

Activity 1: Who's in My Corner?

The people in your circle include friends, family, and colleagues who you interact with regularly. Some of these relationships are a matter of convenience or circumstance, like office or labmates. The people in your corner, however, are those who are invested in you, who are willing to expend energy to support you in different areas of life: academic development, personal development, career development, and more.

In this activity, map out the people who do and will support you in your PhD journey. Use the diagram below to help you identify names in relation to various dimensions of support. If you struggle to find names, consider who you might reach out to in the future. You might jot down current supports inside the box, and potential supporters in the space outside the box.

The primary activity here is for you to walk away having identified your network of support. If there are areas where you would like more supporters, then set that as a goal for yourself. You may need to seek out career mentors or wellness buddies. Try to work toward a balanced support network because throughout your PhD, you will need to rely on relationships across these areas.

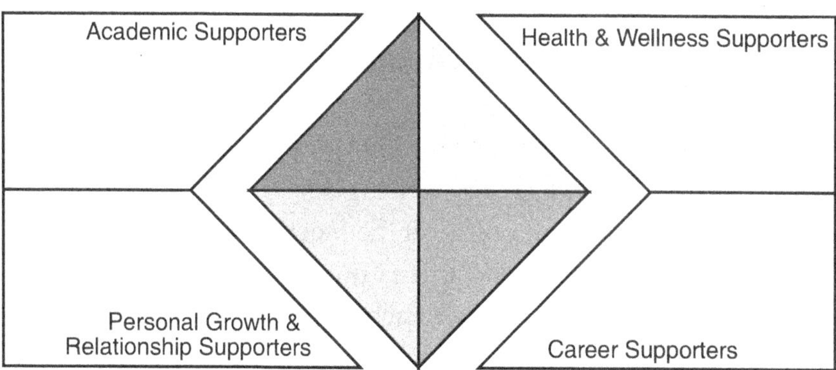
Academic Supporters
Health & Wellness Supporters
Personal Growth &
Relationship Supporters
Career Supporters

Activity 2: In the Aviary – Build Relationships through Intentional Communication

Scenario: Imagine you're in a committee meeting with graduate student and faculty colleagues. An ambitious, direct-to-the-point Eagle starts off the meeting with gusto: "Right, this is our goal, and this is how we are going to get there. We need to act now to achieve results and time is of the essence. Let's go!" An effervescent Peacock says, "That's a great idea – I can promote that right now on my social media accounts; who's with me?" The wise Owl sits back pensively, and when they can get a word in edgewise, says, "Perhaps we should look at all the alternatives; what evidence do we have that this course of action is preferable? We need to slow down." A Dove sits quietly, observing all in the room, and whispers to the colleague next to them, "How does this affect you? I feel uncomfortable with this and think we should make sure we understand how everyone feels about this idea before proceeding."

These four communication styles – Dove, Owl, Peacock, and Eagle – were described by Dr. Gary Couture in the 1970s.

Briefly:

- *Doves* are peaceful, patient, and kind. They tend to be on the quieter side and avoid risk. They also tend toward steady, stable, and supportive.
- *Owls* are conscientious, logical, and detail-oriented. They double check their work and tend toward analysis and skepticism. They want step-by-step, slow decisions

once all the data has been gathered and analyzed. They can be perfectionists and they can be risk averse.

- *Peacocks* love talking! They are enthusiastic, exciting, and excitable. They bring energy to projects and take action, thriving on collaboration. They may strike others as overly optimistic and overly emotional.
- *Eagles* are assertive. They take action and are results-oriented. They thrive on challenge and are competitive and ambitious. They may seem brash and unsympathetic to others.

How can you use the understanding that people communicate differently to enhance your academic relationships?

a. Understand your strengths and weaknesses, and those of others you work with. Do one or more personality tests, paying attention to your scores in all categories. Utilize your strengths and shore up your weaknesses, particularly in conversations with others who have a different communication style. For example – if you are a Dove and you work with an Eagle, recognize that the Eagle values different aspects of relationships and work tasks. Present your ideas in a way that they will hear them effectively, and build trust with others through your kind, patient "superpowers." If you're an Eagle and you work with a Dove, put your assertiveness on hold and listen; collaborate with a Dove to help you develop teams, and bring much-needed stability and conscientiousness to your ambitious goals.

In the table below, list the characteristics where you feel you're strongest and also those where you are weakest. Jot down ways that these characteristics influence *how* you like to communicate and work with others. The first row is done as an example.

Characteristics where I exhibit strength	How this influences how I work with others	Characteristics where I exhibit weakness	How this influences my work with others
e.g., Quick decision-making	e.g., Fast paced and results oriented	e.g., Attention to details	e.g., I might miss details – I might steamroll over those with legitimate concerns

b. Do your best to put yourself in the shoes of others. Do this for your supervisor and others who you work with closely. You will likely find it helpful to review the characteristics of other communication styles to better understand the way they think and work differently. Avoid judging others who think and behave differently than you; instead look to the strengths they bring to the table and create and nurture a productive team. If you can adjust your behaviors and approach, you'll gain trust and work more effectively with others.

Characteristics where my colleague __________ exhibits strength	How this influences their work with me	Characteristics where my colleague ________ exhibits weakness	How this influences their work with me

Activity 3: Meeting Planner Template

Starting meetings with an agenda can be helpful. To assist in communicating effectively with your supervisor(s) and others you may work with, consider using a meeting agenda to provide structure and clarity. An agenda ensures that key topics are prioritized and that discussions remain focused and productive. Use (and adapt) the meeting planner below.

<table>
<tr><td colspan="2">Meeting Topic:</td><td colspan="2">Date:
Start: End:</td></tr>
<tr><td colspan="2">Purpose:</td><td colspan="2">Attendees:
•
•
•</td></tr>
<tr><td colspan="2">Materials to bring:

A/V requirements:</td><td colspan="2">Location:</td></tr>
<tr><td colspan="3">Agenda</td><td>Priority</td></tr>
<tr><td colspan="3"></td><td></td></tr>
<tr><td colspan="3"></td><td></td></tr>
<tr><td colspan="3"></td><td></td></tr>
<tr><td colspan="3"></td><td></td></tr>
<tr><td colspan="3"></td><td></td></tr>
<tr><td colspan="2">Action Items</td><td>Who?</td><td>Deadline</td></tr>
<tr><td colspan="2"></td><td></td><td></td></tr>
<tr><td colspan="2"></td><td></td><td></td></tr>
<tr><td colspan="2"></td><td></td><td></td></tr>
<tr><td colspan="2"></td><td></td><td></td></tr>
<tr><td colspan="4">For next meeting:</td></tr>
</table>

Activity 4: The Three Rs of Reflection

Recall: I Must Remember

What are my top takeaways from this chapter?

Revise: What Do I Want to Do Differently?

Based on the advice from this chapter, what is most important for me to personally change or improve? Write down a commitment for one small action you will do differently right away.

Reimagine: What Do I Hope Will Happen?

Reimagining a future reality for ourselves and setting clear intentions is powerful in changing our current practices and achieving our goals. Based on the advice from this chapter, describe a vision of yourself in the future. A prompt for this exercise: *In one year, I hope …*

CHAPTER FOUR

Manage Your Project

Ah, the life of a doctoral student – navigating a labyrinth of research, delving into complex data analysis, and striving toward the elusive goal of a well-structured thesis. And all that stands between you and success are the time-tested strategies for managing your project, right? Not quite. Project management for a dissertation and doctoral studies more broadly is far more complex than simply deploying a few generic strategies. It requires not only understanding the basics of project management but also tailoring them to the circumstances of academic research and selectively implementing them in ways that respect and bring energy to the ways you work. The various pieces of advice we have compiled illustrate this point – as Brian Chen says, "Good ideas are not as important as how they are executed" – and here, we consider six common themes about how you can make strides in your work while avoiding the all-too-familiar obstacles to progress: (1) planning and scheduling, (2) risk management, (3) time management, (4) communication and collaboration, (5) project management tools, and (6) continuous writing.

Naturally, let's begin with planning and scheduling, which involves developing a roadmap for your research project, punctuated with clearly defined goals and milestones. There are many approaches you might use, but one that many in the project management field point to is the Gantt chart[1,2] (see the example from Dr. MacGregor's doctoral research proposal in the activity section). A Gantt chart is a type of bar chart that illustrates a project schedule and can be easily created in a spreadsheet or with one of the many available project management software options. While a shaded or color-coded Gantt chart might seem excessive, it can be a transformative way to visualize how the various phases of your research flow into one another. As one of us learned, it can also signal to your supervisory committee the need for a conversation about the feasibility and scope of your research. The visual timeline sets out tasks and deadlines, aiding in maintaining focus on what must be accomplished and when. Regardless of whether you use a Gantt chart or some other research planning tool, you will likely find that your plans require continual updating and revising as the uncertain nature of research and life plays out. Even just mapping out the major milestones allows you to control, understand, and plan for when you'll finish. This foresight can prevent the frantic rush to complete an entire thesis in a few months, a situation that, unfortunately, some students find themselves in near the end of their funding. At the same time, as obvious as it may sound, we need to see planning tools for what they are: merely the first of multiple elements that make up a pragmatic approach to managing your dissertation research and doctoral studies.

Next, let's consider risk management, an often-overlooked topic despite the inherent uncertainties in multi-year research projects and programs. What could possibly go awry? In short, everything. From issues with research design (e.g., a recruitment strategy not generating participants), to life developments (e.g., love, babies, caring responsibilities), to unpredictable circumstances outside of your control (e.g., a laptop that suddenly decides it would rather be an expensive paperweight), risks are omnipresent. Where possible, early identification of these potential risks and the development of contingency plans can mitigate minor disruptions from escalating into significant obstacles. Consider the example of your primary data source becoming unexpectedly inaccessible, as was the case for many doctoral students around March 2020. During the early days of the COVID-19 pandemic, countless researchers had to pivot quickly, adapting their methodologies, shifting to online data collection, and finding creative solutions to continue their work under new constraints. For many scientists, lab closures meant their work was completely stalled, with no alternative data sources available. They often turned to writing reviews as a temporary measure, but their primary research was delayed indefinitely. Now, as then, effective risk management requires preparation when possible, adaptation when necessary, and patience when delays are unavoidable. By anticipating and responding to what might go wrong, you can navigate many of the inevitable challenges of your doctoral journey with greater resilience.

The idea of completing your research brings us to the topic of time management. Even the most outwardly "has-it-together" doctoral student will be familiar with the challenge of balancing research with teaching and service responsibilities, personal obligations, and the necessity of rest. Effective time management involves prioritizing tasks, establishing realistic deadlines, and segmenting work into manageable portions to combat procrastination. We've all experienced the last-minute writing marathon with a looming deadline. Yet, empirical evidence has firmly established that such conditions rarely lead to our best efforts, particularly for the highly complex tasks of a doctoral research project. As Berg and Seeber put it in their book *The Slow Professor: Challenging the Culture of Speed in the Academy*, "We need, then, to protect a time and a place for timeless time, and to remind ourselves continually that this is not self-indulgent but rather crucial to intellectual work" (2016, p. 28).[3] Embracing this philosophy, we recognize that creativity requires incubation time. Rather than rushing into tasks, allow time for thinking and reflecting, particularly at the beginning of the doctorate. Writing, being a creative activity, also benefits from this thoughtful approach. It becomes evident that managing time effectively is not just about meeting deadlines but about creating the conditions that allow your best work to emerge, and learning how to do this also takes time.

Equally critical to your progress is effective communication and collaboration with your supervisor and peers. Regular check-ins with your supervisor (and potentially your dissertation committee depending on your program structure) are essential to prevent misunderstandings, receive constructive feedback, and stay aligned with your research objectives. Establishing a routine for communication, whether through scheduled meetings, updates, or collaborative tools, ensures that you remain on track and engaged with your research community. Consider planning who to include in these interactions and forming a writing group for additional support and accountability. Moreover, collaboration extends beyond your supervisor. Engaging with peers can provide additional perspectives, support, and motivation. Academia is a collaborative endeavor, and leveraging the collective knowledge and experience of your network can be incredibly beneficial.

Utilizing project management tools sounds impressive, and indeed they can be – provided you use them effectively. These tools can offer structure and clarity, but there is a caveat. For instance, spending hours perfecting your project timeline in a Gantt chart might seem productive, but it could be eating into valuable research time. The allure of organizing every detail can sometimes overshadow the actual work of conducting research. The key is to find a balance where the tools serve to augment your work without becoming a distraction or a vehicle for procrastination. When used judiciously, task management software helps chart the roadmap of your research, enabling you to stay organized and focused on your objectives.

Finally, an essential strategy is continuous writing. This approach emphasizes the importance of writing regularly rather than striving for perfection in every session. It's less about crafting a masterpiece each day and more about making steady, incremental progress. By writing continuously, you can refine your ideas and document your findings as they emerge, making the final stages of thesis preparation far less daunting. For example, setting aside time each day to write a few hundred words can lead to significant progress over time. Epictetus famously said, "If you wish to be a writer, write," while Dorothy Parker humorously noted that "writing is the art of applying the ass to the seat." Anne Lamott's[4] influential essay *Shitty First Drafts* also highlights the importance of allowing yourself to write imperfectly as a critical part of the creative process.

It's important to acknowledge that the writing phase of the thesis can vary significantly across disciplines. While continuous writing is beneficial for everyone, some fields, such as those involving long-term experiments in the sciences, may not allow for a "write the chapters as you go" model. In these cases, continuous writing can still contribute to the final product by documenting progress, thoughts, and findings throughout the research process. Similarly, some humanities disciplines might require extensive reading and analysis before substantial writing can begin. To plan the writing phase of your thesis effectively, consider an exercise in project management: determine how long you have, estimate the total number of words or chapters needed, and divide the work by the time available to establish a writing pace. This structured approach can help ensure steady progress and prevent last-minute stress. In short, continuous writing helps to keep the momentum going and ensures that the thesis evolves alongside your research.

We have all been there, in the depths of doctoral research, grappling with these very challenges. Yet, through perseverance and strategic adjustments, we managed to navigate the turbulence and emerge with renewed determination. The general suggestions we have discussed and the advice that follows will not provide you with a one-size-fits-all approach; tweak them to suit your unique style and workflow. By using these methods, you may find yourself not only on the path to completing your thesis but doing so with considerably less stress and far more confidence.

ADVICE ON MANAGING YOUR PROJECT

Keep your eyes on the prize. Know that obtaining the PhD is a temporary training period in your life. The process is certainly important and will shape the rest of your life and career, but it is a stepping-stone nonetheless. It doesn't matter if you are not sure about what you want to do after you graduate; either way the goal is still the completion of your PhD. Don't let the uncertainty of your future, or the easy settling of graduate life, be used as an excuse to not move forward toward completion of your PhD. The research that you are doing during your PhD is important, fascinating, inspiring, and beautiful, and this is unrelated to what your career path is after your graduation. Becoming distracted by the beauty of your research field and its unending paths will always be the default choice. We are all dreamers, drawn to solve the mysteries of the unknown, and so I have never worried about the natural curiosity of my graduate students and their desire to explore their field of study. You embark upon a PhD journey because you are a dreamer. But keeping aware of your end goal is important because it trains you to think about the bigger picture and puts your day-to-day work in perspective. Learning how to remain aware of the bigger picture will teach you how to better execute, and this is the most important skill and message I try to instill in my trainees.

Good ideas are not as important as how they are executed. Regardless of the pace of how your research is performed, good execution has never been about how fast you move, but how efficiently you can get things done. Executing an idea well and seeing it all the way through is hard. Try to set concrete goals with three different timelines, aggressive, reasonable, and pessimistic, to visualize and prepare for what that would look like to you. Your research and the natural data will throw their own curveballs, place obstacles, and have their own plans, in addition to your personal life having a say in your timelines. Nevertheless, try to regularly think about what it takes to move forward with every step, and how the little details that you are currently doing fit in with your ultimate goal. Help others get things done. Teach others how to get things done, by solving problems and executing efficiently. If you learn how to execute well, in solving problems, overcoming obstacles, and moving forward efficiently, this will be the most important skill you hone during your PhD.

Brian Chen,

McGill University, Neuroscience

Doing a thesis is a long journey that can seem overwhelming. It is probably the only project that a doctoral student has done on such a large scale. The complexity and scope of the work are initially hard to comprehend. There are many pieces of advice, all valuable, but I have found that having students develop a timeline or schedule helps them break the thesis process into manageable chunks and it also keeps them accountable. Visually seeing the entire doctoral process makes it less scary. I give my students a handout of the required steps.

Since students will be working on the project for years, they feel like they have the luxury of time but it is so easy to let time float away. Often they are reading extensively for their literature review, which is often a form of procrastination – delaying starting to write. When I start with a new doctoral student we create a schedule for their coursework which is often the easiest part of the doctoral process. Included in that discussion is figuring out which days of the week or evening they can devote to reading and writing for their coursework. This gets them into the habit of scheduling their writing. Once the coursework is done we do a timeline for the next stage, which includes completing their comprehensive exam, writing their proposal, and obtaining ethical approval. Once those three steps are done we do another timeline for data gathering and analysis. This is a month-by-month plan which allows me to see if they understand the data gathering process – what is involved? Often students wildly underestimate how long it will take to gather data. At our regular check ins (biweekly/monthly) I require them to bring the schedule and we adjust as needed and discuss why they are not on track. This is an easy way to open conversations about feeling nervous, family or financial issues, and I can see if they are spending too much time on other tasks (e.g., such as being a research assistant: Are they exceeding the number of required hours?). Breaking down such an enormous task into manageable pieces allows students to check off each accomplishment, which is motivating.

Clare Kosnik,
University of Toronto, Education

Journey. Process. Reflection. These three words are behaviors in action that PhD students should embrace. A PhD program is a journey and it is critical to appreciate the daily nuances of it. A PhD program is a series of processes and steps. View each process (e.g., completing papers, presenting at conferences, GTA duties) in smaller manageable pieces, rather than focusing on everything and becoming overwhelmed. A paper is so much more interesting when we have researched and written it with a plan in mind (e.g., writing two to three pages a day for ten days and then revisiting it). Reflection embodies the ability to look at what is working and removing what doesn't. It means we have the courage to do things differently.

Pamela Rose Toulouse,
Laurentian University, Education

Do not ignore inadequate research progress over a significant period of time. At periodic intervals, for example once a year, you must make an honest assessment of your rate of progress. If it is inadequate, meaning that it will not enable you to complete your thesis project in the desired time frame, then you must be prepared to address this. Some decisions may have to be made that will be crucial to the success of your project. First, you should ensure that you are working sufficiently hard and effectively and have not started exploiting the freedom and absence of regular milestones often associated with graduate studies. That may be the first thing to correct. Perhaps you need more regular meetings with your advisor. Next you and your advisor must assess whether your project needs to be changed in order to address the lack of progress. This can be a very difficult decision. You definitely do not want to give up on an idea prematurely, but you also do not want to invest more and more time in something that is not destined to bear fruit. There are no magical answers in such cases, but it is important that a rational decision be made after an assessment of research progress, as opposed to simply continuing down a particular path without recognizing that progress is inadequate. Often a key to a successful research project is recognizing relatively quickly that a direction is flawed, and determining how to reorient the project, presumably based on what has been learned.

David Zingg,
University of Toronto, Computational Aerodynamics

Typically, doctoral students are motivated to write a strong proposal and collect data. Many students, however, avoid writing the final dissertation because the process is lonely and because they believe their writing isn't good enough. If you believe you might have this difficulty, ask your supervisor to provide structure and deadlines. Think about your own style and circumstances. Are you more productive if you write intensively (e.g., for twelve hours per day for a period of a few months) or if you write for an hour daily for a year or two. If you are struggling to write, speak to your supervisor; it is very difficult to support a student who disappears and does not respond.

Judy Wiener,
University of Toronto,
Psychology and Human Development

The most important behavior PhD students should avoid is without any doubt avoiding the writing. One of the hardest and most time-consuming parts of a PhD is to write the final thesis. It is the time to put everything together, the results of tenuous experiments, the long hours of reading, and the countless thought processes. It is an intimidating process for many, and a gigantic process for others. Writer's block can be an overwhelming feeling. The secret is to start writing day 1: write each literature review, write each result as they come by, write each thought process, etc. And then when the time comes, putting all this together will be much easier, since everything will be already there, ready to be used and processed. Writing is an exercise that requires continuous training. It can transform into a passion if well nurtured with awareness and patience.

Pia Wintermark,
McGill University, Pediatrics

Naturally there are many crucial elements to completing a PhD to a high standard and within the length of the program: good time-keeping, developing field knowledge, a clear central thesis, an appropriate advisory team, good peer relationships, and strong personal resilience are just a few of the skills and support mechanisms needed to do a doctorate well. But I would venture that structure and flexibility are the most crucial components. Balancing these applies to both a doctoral scholar's approach to his or her daily work and to the overall design and development of the thesis itself. The PhD journey is a long one and candidates should quickly determine a basic structure for their daily, weekly, and monthly work, with an overall sense of what the thesis will look like in the end. At the same time, candidates also need to recognize that any such plan must be subject to constant adjustment and flux, as new ideas are generated through the research process and the overarching design changes to accommodate a developing sense of the central claims. Most of us tend to orient more comfortably in one direction or another, as planners or more tractable thinkers, more or less inclined toward working in structured or flexible ways. PhD students need to find a balance to ensure they produce a timely, original, and well-organized thesis that benefits from both ways of thinking and researching.

Zoe Jaques,
University of Cambridge, Children's Literature

Give yourself TIME – time to read, time to do experiments, time to write your thesis. Don't underestimate how long it takes to do a good job (and probably avoid looking to your professors for good examples of time management!).

Emma Allen-Vercoe,
University of Guelph, Molecular and Cell Biology

Crucial to your success in graduate school is your ability to develop good writing habits. It's easy to think that you need to do more research before you start writing that seminar paper, that prospectus draft, that dissertation chapter. But "I need to do more reading" too easily becomes procrastination. So stop reading, and start writing. Moving beyond mantra, here are some more concrete suggestions. Figure out if you're a morning or night person, and then make that your time to write. Set aside time each day for writing – put it in your calendar and guard it like treasure. Realize that you can get good work done even if you only have an hour to write. Learn to impose deadlines on yourself: commit, for instance, to submitting a paper to a conference or agree to present a thesis chapter at a "work-in-progress" session. Form a writing group as a way to both get feedback on your work and hold yourself accountable for making progress on your dissertation. Get comfortable deleting what you wrote: you can do better.

Charlie Kurth,
Clemson University, Philosophy

Avoid falling into the cyclical trap of believing your drafts must be perfect before submitting or that supervisor feedback is criticism of you personally, and then using either as an excuse not to submit work, or worse, ceasing to write altogether.

During the inevitable rough patches in a PhD journey – when life's challenges intersect with academic demands – try to keep writing, even if it's just two hundred words a day. This manageable goal not only keeps you engaged, but also helps mitigate feelings of being overwhelmed and the looming expectation of perfection in each draft. Consistent, small efforts accumulate and can significantly overcome what may initially seem like insurmountable obstacles.

Remember that feedback is not a judgment of your abilities or value but is intended to guide and refine your work. Academics, often pressed for time, typically focus their reviews on areas for improvement. This doesn't mean they undervalue your efforts; rather, it reflects a common academic practice of entering "marking mode," where the emphasis is on correction rather than commendation. I experienced this firsthand with my own PhD supervisor, who frequently returned my work extensively marked in red pen – even drafts that had already undergone multiple rounds of revision. I did not realize at the time that the nature of the feedback I was receiving was evolving as I incorporated his suggestions and improved: I just saw red pen. This misunderstanding led me to wonder whether my supervisor regretted taking me on. My perspective only shifted when I accidentally discovered a reference my supervisor wrote on my PhD completion revealing their regard for my work.

Feelings of not being good enough, of not belonging, and of intellectual fraudulence are pervasive in academia: it's likely your supervisor relates to these feelings too and has their own stories. Openly discussing these thoughts and feelings with others (students and academics) can help normalize such fears and foster a more supportive environment. This, in turn, makes it easier to persist and engage with the writing process, submit drafts more freely, ask questions, and view all feedback as an opportunity to learn and grow – after all, this is what the PhD process is all about.

Elizabeth R. Peterson,
University of Auckland, Psychology

The best dissertation is a done one. It is a simple maxim but one to live by during your PhD journey. Too often students are overwhelmed or paralyzed by the dissertation as a whole or individual steps along the way. They think it has to be groundbreaking, revolutionary, and transformative. Don't let it loom so large in front of you that it casts shadows of doubt in your mind. Cut it down to size.

Approach the dissertation for what is – a demonstrative task. It is not your life's work but rather an opportunity to demonstrate that you understand how to design, conduct, analyze, and disseminate scholarly research that makes a contribution to your field.

It is not the last thing you will ever write or even the most important! It is more likely the first. Think for a moment. Have you read all the dissertations of the leading scholars in your field? Probably not. Your thinking will change from what you write in your dissertation – and, rightly so! It should evolve! You will keep learning more information, develop new inquiry skills, and encounter new people, theories, and technologies throughout your career – but, you can't get there unless you finish the dissertation.

So, design a manageable inquiry that fascinates you. To the extent possible, enjoy learning and practicing the skills you need to establish a solid foundation for your career. The PhD is not your career – it is the launch pad. Your research career is the rocket. Don't confuse the two.

The dissertation is not the cumulation of your life's work. You will collect more data than you need. You don't have to put it all in your dissertation. Your job is to find the research story and learn how to tell it well. Then, get it done so you can get on with living your best (academic) life.

Gail Prasad,
York University, Education

Avoid writing badly. Understand well how to write with good style; read Don Knuth's *Mathematical Writing*; understand English grammar well. Don't use key constructs badly, such as which/that, use/utilize, like/such as. Avoid using the impersonal passive voice, write directly and clearly. Remember the purpose of writing is not to dump the contents of your brain onto paper; it is to transfer your thinking to the reader's brain, so write for the reader not the author. Don't be drawn in to continual editing by the text editor; print your draft writing on paper and sit far away from your computer to read and mark up your text; under a shady tree is a good place.

Bruce MacDonald,
University of Auckland, Engineering

Undertaking and eventually completing a PhD program is an incredibly rewarding experience but it can also be a very "hard slog." To ensure that the experience is rewarding

I recommend that incoming students do some preparatory work to make sure the topic of their thesis really interests them, that they have mapped out a series of experiments or studies that thematically fit together, and that the group or laboratory in which they will be based has the facilities and resources available to ensure the work is feasible. Although this might sound obvious, many students do not start their PhD with a clear roadmap of where they will go. A clear roadmap will help keep the student on track, particularly when they encounter the inevitable bumps in the road. A genuine interest in the topic and a belief that the whole undertaking is worthwhile and meaningful for the student, academia, and society in general will help the student thrive.

Mark Bellgrove,
Monash University, Cognitive Neuroscience

My single most important piece of advice to a doctoral researcher would be to prioritize the formulation of a plan for the full length of the candidature and include major milestones. The plan should be made right at the start of the candidature. Revisiting that plan regularly – the revisits would be scheduled in the plan! – as the work progresses will result in more detail being added and the plan would thus be fleshed out along the way. Such a plan, and a routine process of revisiting it, helps both the student and the supervisors keep their eyes on the overall goal, while also providing the student with assurance that the work can be done. Assurance is necessary, as any big piece of work can feel overwhelming at times. A good plan can serve as the foundation, holding the candidature firmly on track, freeing and enabling the student to delve into the work that needs to be done along the way. It can therefore help them to take one step at a time, to give their energies over to tackling the challenges that come with each step. The plan provides the confidence that is often needed to assist a doctoral researcher to see the relevance and contribution of each small step to the achievement of the overall goal of completing the research and producing the thesis. Such a plan would of course be formulated in collaboration and with assistance of supervisors. It becomes a focus of discussion, reflection, and evaluation for the supervisory group and therefore brings with it many benefits for everyone involved, but particularly for the student.

Sarah Stein,
University of Otago, Education

Start writing from the outset. This might seem odd, especially among those still using the outdated language of a "writing up" period, but it's essential if the thesis is to emerge as a mature, accomplished piece of writing. Writing throughout the process of researching a PhD enables you to develop the skill of academic writing, and it is a skill, one that demands long-term investment and fine-tuning. Ask any established academic, and they'll tell you that their writing has improved over their career as they have acquired more experience and refined their craft. It stands to reason, therefore, that we cannot begin writing in earnest halfway or two thirds of the way through a PhD and expect the final product to be the best we could have accomplished. Start early, and the writing has more time to evolve, to improve, and to enable the thesis to rise to a higher academic standard.

A further advantage is you have something concrete and substantial to discuss with your supervisor when you meet. More informal chats can be helpful, but experience suggests if these become the norm, a lot less is achieved in that precious hour than could have been had a few thousand words of a draft chapter been the focus of the conversation.

Aside from these practical considerations, writing early also recognizes that the distinction between "research" and "writing" is a false one. We need to move beyond the old, rather clunky model that imagines research and writing to exist as linear stages in a flow chart, as if writing a thesis was a bit like baking a cake. Get the order wrong and you end up with an indigestible product and probably a very messy kitchen. PhDs are definitely messy, but they don't work like this. Writing is an integral part of the research, chiefly because achieving the discursive expression of your argument is how you clarify and demonstrate your thinking. Simply put: writing well is thinking well. Revising, editing, reflecting, and rewriting is not just about putting preformulated ideas on the page; it's about developing those thoughts. Writing about the topic you're researching is the principal means by which you will make sense of it. This means you'll have a lot on the cutting room floor by the time you're done, but your thesis will be a much, much stronger piece of academic work as a consequence.

Mathew Guest,
Durham University, Sociology of Religion

Do not leave things to the last minute – your deadline is not your supervisor's problem. Let your supervisor know when things don't work but also when they do, as this brings good energy. Don't avoid bad news, as your supervisor needs to know where you are at – evasive students don't do well. Try to schedule regular sessions so stuff does not pile up.

Beate Kampmann,
London School of Hygiene & Tropical Medicine,
Infectious and Tropical Diseases

It is probably fairly obvious, but the most destructive behavior for doctoral scholars is procrastination. Naturally everyone puts off difficult bits of writing or reading uninspiring research papers now and again, but sustained periods of inactivity can be very difficult to recover from and have heralded the end of many a thesis. In terms of the overall calendar of a doctoral journey, the length of a PhD can stretch before candidates and give a false impression of endless time. Doctoral programs are lengthy because there is a great deal of necessary work to do, and it is crucial that candidates allocate proper time to their research and exercise consistent working habits. Even if there are periods in which students cannot maintain their usual pace, it is good practice to make sure that they read something relevant (however short) or write something germane to their research (even notes) every day. It is a cliché to say that a PhD is a marathon not a sprint, but it is important to keep in mind that attempts to write a PhD quickly "at the end" rarely do justice to the research. It is also crucial that students seek appropriate support and guidance anytime they feel significant anxiety relating to the PhD; it is very common for procrastination to occur as a symptom of researchers' negative self-reflection on their own abilities and the overwhelming nature of the task at hand. "Imposter syndrome" is widespread in the PhD (and in academia at large) and it is important to seek reassurance and guidance from advisory teams and wider support networks to combat such damaging negativity should it arise.

Zoe Jaques,
University of Cambridge, Children's Literature

The obvious advice is the most important but also the very hardest to give and to receive and that is, to write all the time and as much as possible. Writing a one-hundred-thousand-word thesis is such a formidable exercise that it's often the thing that acts as the biggest figurative, emotional, and physical barrier. When we're trying to find our voice, even putting pen to paper is so very, very hard. But one thing is for sure – you're never going to find your voice if you don't actually write anything, and that's for two important reasons. First, because there literally won't be any tangible artifact in which a voice can present itself. But secondly, our voice only begins to emerge and shine as we speak it, write it, repeat it in a thousand different ways, but above all, see it growing before our eyes. So, forget about creating a comfortable sitting space, a protected writing space, a conducive to thinking space; the best space is any space, and any space is writing space, whether on a table, a tablet, a diary, or a desk. Everything can be edited, shaped, cultivated, disciplined, but it can't be if it's just not there. So just write, and write every day, wherever and whenever.

Caroline Walker-Gleaves,
Newcastle University, Education

REFLECTION AND APPLICATION ACTIVITIES

"Good ideas are not as important as how they are executed," advises Brian Chen. This chapter is about the nuts and bolts of getting a PhD completed. The advice has two main themes: time management to ensure this long journey has the right magic combination of "structure and flexibility" as Zoe Jaques puts it, and that the key task of writing is not avoided, but rather intentionally developed as a regular activity. Whether you are a planner, procrastinator, or something in between, Chart the Milestones! uses a fundamental project management tool to help you get a grasp of the big picture and proceed with your journey in full awareness of your progress.

Writing stands out, in the minds of these top supervisors, as a difficult, and crucial, component of the graduate student's skill set and activities. To help establish the writing habit, and foster awareness of the time management system that works best for you, we offer Takt – The Rhythm of Writing to a Deadline. Whether you write a snippet of your dissertation every day or have a writing period at the end, use this tool to understand how you can best set and meet your writing goals. And, finally, the Writing Prescription will guide decisions to cement into daily routines the habits that bring you success.

Activity 1: Chart the Milestones!

Map out your doctorate program in three-month increments. If you're well along in the process, it's never too late!

- Add the years to the column headings.
- Add columns as necessary for programs longer than three years.
- Adjust the major activities to suit your own project: for example, if obtaining ethical clearance will be a long process for you, or if the nature of your project precludes you from writing individual manuscripts in phases, but rather requires longer periods of time for holistic writing at the end. In this case, your phases might look like:
  - Formulate research question/project plan
  - Gather data
  - Analyze data
  - Write dissertation
- Rough out how long you need for each phase, paying attention to activities that must be done before another can start – what's known in project management as "dependencies." Many doctoral programs outline the timing for major milestones in a graduate handbook. This is a good place to start as you build your chart.

You'll want to replicate this chart in a spreadsheet or project management software so that you can make adjustments and track your progress over time. Stephen's Gantt chart appears on the next page as an example, followed by a generic Gantt chart for you to use.

Stephen MacGregor's PhD Gantt Chart

Phases and Major Activities	2019		2020				2021			
	Jul-Sep	Oct-Dec	Jan-Mar	Apr-Jun	Jul-Sep	Oct-Dec	Jan-Mar	Apr-Jun	Jul-Sep	Oct-Dec
1: Scoping Review & Environmental Scan										
Scoping: Identify / select relevant literature										
Scoping: Chart data, collate, summarize, and report findings										
Write Manuscript 1										
Environmental Scan: Collect documents										
Environmental Scan: Analyze document content										
2: Interviews & Case Selection										
Contact internal RIC actors for recruitment										
Conduct interviews										
Transcribe interview data										
Analyze interview data										
Write Manuscript 2										
Selection of co-production cases Phase 3										
3: Landscape Interviews & Survey										
Contact research services informants for recruitment										
Conduct interviews										
Transcribe/analyze interview data										
Re-analysis institutional documents from Phase 1 – context analysis										
Write Manuscript 3										
Survey development										
Survey deployment										
Survey analysis										
Write Manuscript 4										
Dissertation Finalizing										
Write final chapter synthesize contributions of each manuscript										
Write introductory chapter										
Review time for Committee										
Defend										

Generic Gantt Chart

Phases and Major Activities	20__				20__				20__			
	Jan-Mar	Apr-Jun	Jul-Sep	Oct-Dec	Jan-Mar	Apr-Jun	Jul-Sep	Oct-Dec	Jan-Mar	Apr-Jun	Jul-Sep	Oct-Dec
Phase 1: Formulating Question/Planning Project												
Literature Review												
Research Proposal												
Ethics/legal review												
Phase 2:												
Phase 3:												
Phase 4:												
Defend												

Activity 2: Takt – The Rhythm of Writing to a Deadline

The German word "Takt" means beat or pulse in music. Lean management principles apply the term "Takt time" to describe the rate at which you need to complete a product in order to meet demand. Essentially, planning your dissertation writing phase requires an understanding of pace, so you know how much writing you need to produce per unit of time in order to meet a chosen deadline. This worksheet provides strategies to figure out how much time you need to write a project.

Part 1: Know Your Natural Writing Pace

(If your dissertation includes complex figures, video, or other elements, the same principle applies – you need to know how much you can get done in a given period of time.)

Decide on a time frame for your writing session, in hours. Will you be able to write comfortably every day for eight hours or is seven hours more reasonable? Perhaps you are working part-time and can only write for four hours at a time.	#hours in writing session:
Test how much you can produce in that time frame. You want to make sure it is an average session, not a super productive one. You want to eat lunch, check your email, make tea, and do all the other non-work-related activities you do in an average day. Measure the production in words or pages. Some can write two thousand draft words a day. Ernest Hemingway wrote five hundred words a day, from 9:00 a.m.–2:00 p.m.	#words/pages in an average writing session:
Alternatively, you can test how much you can produce in a time frame by choosing a small task – a complex figure, a chapter introduction, a full chapter, etc. Do the identified tasks and note how many hours each takes you.	#hours per additional task: #sessions per task:
The average PhD thesis is two hundred to three hundred pages, but this differs with discipline and program. You need to estimate how many words or pages, roughly, you have to write. You'll want to add time for figures, references, etc. Talk to your supervisor and check comparable peer dissertations in your department to get a decent estimate of the size of a finished thesis.	#total words/pages to write:
Number of days/sessions required to finish thesis: #words/pages in an average writing session + #sessions per #total words/pages left to write additional task	#days/sessions of writing required for first draft:
Now that you have the # of days/sessions, you need to translate that to a deadline. How many days/sessions a week can you write? Perhaps it's a five-day work week, or perhaps you're in a hurry and it's a six-day week – but don't try to work more than six days per week writing a large project – you'll detract from your quality; you need time to rejuvenate.	#weeks until first draft:
You also need to allow extra time for unforeseen circumstances, such as illness or other obligations. Suggestion: two days a month.	#days/sessions of writing required = #weeks (+ extra time) × #days/ sessions per week.

Part 2: Two Ways to Meet Your Daily Target

Keeping on pace day after day is a challenge on its own! There are two tried and true methods, one of which will likely work better for you than the other. Try both to find out which method you'll use to stay on track.

Pace Yourself by # of Words	Pace Yourself by Time
Write until you've met your daily word count and then quit. This is a favorite method because • When you're finished, sometimes early, sometimes a little later – you know you're on pace and can take time off, stress-free. There's a competitive challenge embedded to finish early and be rewarded with more time off.	Many writers manage their writing progress with a kitchen timer, involving fully focused bursts of writing punctuated by brief rests for the brain and body. Called the "Pomodoro technique," start with twenty-five minutes of focused writing and a five-minute break, then repeat.
• On tough days, when you're two hundred words off your target, you'll keep going and often get some wind in your sails and fly past the target, putting words in your bank, which alleviates stress.	You might also try forty-five minutes of focus and fifteen minutes of break. What matters is that you're cycling focus and break time. With this method, you can figure out quickly how much time you need to focus each day to reach your daily output target.

Activity 3: Writing Prescription

This activity will help you successfully develop the habit of writing regularly and frequently. If you are not sure about your responses, experiment to figure out what works best for you. You won't regret it.

<table>
<tr><th colspan="2">Writing Prescription</th></tr>
<tr><td>Best time of day:</td><td>❑ Early morning ❑ Lunchtime ❑ After work
❑ Late morning ❑ Afternoon ❑ After dinner</td></tr>
<tr><td>Best location:</td><td>❑ Home office ❑ Library ❑ Couch
❑ Work office ❑ Cafe ❑ Other: ______</td></tr>
<tr><td>Consistency/Variety</td><td>❑ I benefit from consistent environment and time
❑ I benefit from varying environment and time</td></tr>
<tr><td colspan="2">Best strategy if stuck or interrupted:
❑ Talking my thoughts out ❑ Doing something physical
❑ Making a list of tasks to do ❑ Editing previous work
❑ Free writing for 5 minutes ❑ Taking a nap
❑ Reading to stimulate ideas ❑ Using a writing prompt
❑ Seeking feedback ❑ Other: ______________</td></tr>
<tr><td colspan="2">Resources required to maintain focus:
❑ Books/articles ❑ Fidget activity ❑ Music/headphones
❑ Turn off phone ❑ Turn off email ❑ Turn off social media
❑ Other: ______________________________</td></tr>
<tr><td colspan="2">My plan for writing frequently and regularly is....</td></tr>
</table>

Activity 4: The Three Rs of Reflection

Recall: I Must Remember

What are my top takeaways from this chapter?

Revise: What Do I Want to Do Differently?

Based on the advice from this chapter, what is most important for me to personally change or improve? Write down a commitment for one small action you will do differently right away.

Reimagine: What Do I Hope Will Happen?

Reimagining a future reality for ourselves and setting clear intentions is powerful in changing our current practices and achieving our goals. Based on the advice from this chapter, describe a vision of yourself in the future. A prompt for this exercise: *In one year, I hope …*

CHAPTER FIVE

Seek Balance

We are constantly told to keep everything in balance – food, stress, work, spending, and even fun … lest we get too obsessed with fun! In a world that seems to have gotten itself so far out of balance – from polarizing politics to massive climate changes to 24/7 email cycles to our epidemic screen fixation – it is no wonder that the sage advice to seek balance is so alluring. And yet, for many, it remains elusive. Despite the prolific talk of balance in our societies, it seems that very few actually achieve it. Why? Has society become hardwired against balance?

Celeste Headlee in her book *Do Nothing: How to Break Away from Overworking, Overdoing, and Underliving*[1] traces how the industrial age established new expectations for work, displacing leisure, family, and other balancing activities. The caution in her book, which we have seen play out time and time again in many of our lives, is that when we displace balancing activities, our well-being is displaced too: stress rises, performance decreases, and burnout inevitably triumphs. Headlee advocates the need to rediscover leisure activities: to invest in idling, socializing, and perhaps most importantly to stop comparing our achievements and calendars to others'. This is useful advice, which we can all heed, but how does it work within the constraints of a PhD, where the time-to-complete clock ticks daily, funding wanes, comparison to others is a key metric of success, and there is a constant explicit pressure to publish more and with increased impact?

What does it mean to seek balance along the doctoral journey? More to the point, is balance even attainable while completing a PhD? Albert Einstein is famously quoted as saying, "Life is like riding a bicycle. To keep your balance, you must keep moving." The same is true when riding in the PhD lane. Of course, the PhD bicycle tends to have more wheels, lots of gears, and at times feels like there are more than a few riders on board. It is more akin to riding a ten-speed, quadruplet pentacycle than your regular ride-in-the-park two-wheeler.

On the one hand, pursuing a doctorate might appear to be a lifestyle that enables, if not encourages, balance. From the outside, it looks like a PhD allows a person to freely pursue their passion, with ample time and resources, and the autonomy to set their own schedule, balancing academic work with other life priorities. For some PhDers, this idyllic version of the doctoral journey holds true. For others, however, perhaps the majority, the PhD looks more like juggling precarious part-time jobs (teaching assistantships, research assistantships, and other employment) with coursework, comprehensive exams, and a dissertation. Living on a shoestring budget often in a new city away from family and friends. Raising families and caring for elderly family members. Planning for what seems to be an ever-tightening job market. Imposter syndrome. Constant feedback from supervisors, committee members, and external reviewers. Staggered successes coupled with what often feels like constant rejection. Some have said that the P in PhD stands for *perseverance*. Completing a PhD undeniably requires will, self-regulation, and resilience.

Research into the lives of PhD students shows that, for many, balance is a distant reality. Doctoral students face challenges balancing academic demands and program obligations with social and family responsibilities, often neglecting personal life goals, leading to escalating social isolation and deficits in positive emotions.[2] The result is delays in progress, higher levels of burnout and intentions to drop out, and lower well-being.[3,4] Yet the research is also clear that the converse is true. Satisfaction with work-life balance is positively linked with higher motivation, self-efficacy and satisfaction with doctoral studies, and lower drop out intentions.[5,6] Accordingly, there is a need to support doctoral students in achieving balance and engagement in life beyond the academy. There is a need to support doctoral students in nurturing all aspects of their well-being – social, physical, spiritual, financial, and emotional – so that they can thrive intellectually and creatively.

But how to achieve this? We think Einstein got it right with his analogy of the bike: "To keep your balance, you must keep moving." It's physics: moving forward prevents us from falling. The same is true when doing a PhD. We fall off the bike when we procrastinate or when we get discouraged by negative feedback or rejection from a journal or being isolated from others. Of course, there are other factors that can hoist us from our bikes, too. Whatever the cause of our fall, the key is to get back on and keep moving forward – not just with our academic work but with our social, family, and personal goals and commitments too – to keep moving forward *in balance*. While "moving forward" can (and likely should) involve processing why we have fallen off our bike (e.g., why we are procrastinating or feeling discouraged), it also means finding tangible and practical strategies to start writing or revising or resubmitting again. One of our favorite quotes, which is posted above one of our desks, is "in order to start, you must start." It is simple and true, and applies to just about anything: academic work, eating well, working out, or having more fun! The challenge lies in finding the spark of motivation to start.

Some will say that motivation is about transforming tiny habits in daily practice.[7] If you want to start working out, start by just putting on your running shoes each day. Then, put on your shoes and go outside. Then put on your shoes, go outside, and go for a five-minute walk. And so on until you have established a habit of running each day. This strategy of building tiny habits into bigger ones, which ultimately form routines, is a good one that is supported by psychological research.[8] But the seed of this change lies in realizing the motivation for starting to transform the tiny habit in the first place. For example, if a doctoral student is struggling to write due to a bad case of writer's block, what helps to motivate them to take that first step and open a new Word document on their computer?

Motivation is fundamentally about small sparks and big dreams. The small sparks are the rewards and pleasures that ignite us each day to get us going and moving forward. When we are purposeful about the small sparks, they can also keep us in balance on a daily basis. Small sparks are unique to each person. For us, one small spark is striking a task off the "things to do" list. Ice cream is another small spark. It is good to identify your small sparks as they can help motivate your daily routine and initiate transformations in your tiny habits. Importantly, and as the research on doctoral education tells us, if your small sparks can be social and relational, they will be more effective at keeping you balanced. Using social and family relationships and commitments as small sparks helps people to balance life and work. One action you can take (and which is reflected in the activities at the end of this chapter) is to identify the mini rewards – the sparks – that motivate you to find balance across the physical, social, emotional, and spiritual dimensions of life. Seek out the sparks that invite you to reconnect with people and nature, forge deeper relationships, relax, and move away from your screens or lab bench.

Ultimately, however, your will and resilience to complete your PhD over the long haul is driven by your big dreams. Interestingly, in talking with many PhD students, it is surprising how many do not have a clear vision of their big dream – a connection to why they are doing their PhD and where they envision it leading them. Taking time to draw out and articulate your vision for your post-PhD life can be highly motivating. The clarity that comes with this exercise helps guide your decisions, work priorities, and scholarly habits. For many, it can also help reset expectations around work and prioritize engagement with family and friends. Reminding yourself of your big dreams helps you, especially when you feel like you are pedaling uphill, and the plateau is nowhere in sight.

What does all this talk about motivation, sparks, and dreams have to do with seeking balance? If you know where you want to go and what your priorities are, you can begin to live your life in a way that is congruent (read: in balance) with those priorities. Balance will look different for everyone. What is essential is defining and understanding what balance means for you. One of the most profound lessons academics often learn years after their tenure is that the habits they developed in their PhD – how they learn to work as a scholar – are the habits they carry with them into their career and life. If you want to have time and space for meaningful engagement with family and friends in your post-PhD life, or leisure or fitness activities, then you need to develop these habits now. The PhD is a habit-forming journey, and this chapter calls you to form habits that are in balance with your priorities. The remaining advice in this chapter shares strategies, some practical and others more abstract, to help you set balance-seeking intentions and practices in motion, as Einstein would have you do. Clear within the advice is that while seeking balance may be a continuous pursuit, and a challenging one, it is necessary for establishing healthy, longstanding scholarly habits to sustain you throughout your PhD and beyond.

ADVICE ON SEEKING BALANCE

Balance is a word that is often not associated with the life of a PhD student, and I fully believe that it is the most critical. Balance means that each individual has to have a strategic and purposeful plan on how to be well physically, emotionally, intellectually, and spiritually. PhD students are immersed in the intellectual aspect of their lives, but this cannot reach its full potential without a holistic approach. The intellectual refers to coursework, comprehensive exams, proposal defenses, GTAs, conferences, publications, and the many other parts of this domain in the PhD life. However, investing time and energy in the physical, emotional, and spiritual is equally important to being effective and efficient. The physical is eating well (as opposed to living on caffeine), sleeping well, and getting time outside. The emotional is having a support network of family, friends, and activities that nurture the heart. The spiritual refers to engaging in conversations, events, and practices that promote deep connections with others and something greater than the self. So, for me, BALANCE is the pursuit and fulfillment of a PhD program that has impact for the student and the community around them.

Pamela Rose Toulouse,
Laurentian University, Education

Find balance. Balance should be thought of on a daily timeline in terms of balancing work, self, and family obligations. Exercise, sleep, eat healthy foods, and be social (if you're an extrovert like me): these are all things that will make your work better and your work time more efficient. Have goals both inside and outside of school. For example, I ran my first (and only) marathon while in grad school. As a full professor, I started taking piano lessons.

While we should strive for balance on a daily basis, there are regular rhythms of the semester and conference deadlines which occasionally may make this difficult. Balance may get thrown off for a few days here and there. It happens. Just get back to it as soon as you can. The key is to achieve balance in the long term, whether that be finishing the PhD or getting tenure. You need balance to ensure you can thrive over a lifetime.

Lee Humphreys,
Cornell University, Communications

Don't work seven days a week. Each week take a day off (for me it is Saturdays) and do something different on that day to recharge your mental batteries. You must be in good physical shape too because "Healthy Body = Healthy Mind." So, please don't be a couch potato and do something physical a few days a week; go jogging (as I have been doing), go for brisk walks, or go swimming. Physical exercise allows you to think clearly; would you believe it, I remember proving a theorem while I was jogging.

Sometimes you may experience a mental block for a brief period of a few weeks (or maybe, a month or so) and you get stuck in proving a theorem or analyzing your data. This is common in our business, so don't lose hope and don't give up quickly. Remember that when we embark on a research project, we normally don't see the light at the end of the tunnel, and it may take several attempts to get the desired results. But, if your mental block continues for many months and you are not getting any results, then it is time to consider abandoning that particular project after consulting with your supervisor. You have to finish your PhD in four (or five) years, so don't waste time on projects that are not going anywhere.

Mahmut Parlar,
McMaster University, Management

Like any new relationship, writing a PhD thesis is a big adventure. There are new and exciting aspects to your partner the more you get involved with it. This kind of devotion is essential to persevere, but it should not take complete hold of you and lead you into a labyrinth of endless possibilities. Remind yourself of your guiding questions constantly. Avoid following every seemingly promising new aspect of your project just because it seems so exciting and irresistible to you if it does not help you answer your central question. Keep all the additional ideas and material you have collected for later research, because there will be a life after this Lebensabschnittspartnerschaft.[9]

Lovestruck couples sometimes have a tendency to withdraw into their relationship and not care about the rest of the world anymore. Doctoral research can become a very lonely and isolating experience. Try to avoid that and keep an interest in what is happening around you. You will need the dedication for your project. That is the priority of your life during the Lebensabschnittspartnerschaft but do not dive too deep into it. Avoid forgetting to take a break and mingle and have a party every now and then. It will refresh you and your partner.

Stefan Rinke,
Freie Universität Berlin, History of Latin America

Don't lose yourself to the work. Graduate studies can be extraordinarily difficult and trying. It is important to have the support of friends and family and to take care of your physical and mental health. A source of leisure to relieve your mind of your project is also essential. For me, it was whitewater kayaking. When approaching a rapid, my mind was blissfully not filled with calculations. Others have reported finding refuge in music, cooking, rock climbing, video games, bridge, and even baking and decorating intricate cakes.

Jason Metcalfe,
University of North Carolina at Chapel Hill, Mathematics

Avoid saying "yes" to things, even if they are interesting and creative, unless they fit your own agenda for the program. University campuses are full of exciting opportunities and there is no doubt that a student should take advantage of what is available while there. That said, doctoral programs make tough demands on your time, so it is important to establish one or two clear goals and set them as a priority. This way you can agree to do things that will keep you on the trajectory of fulfilling those goals and you can turn down other opportunities without guilt or remorse. This sounds easier than it is. There will be pressure to get another paper published, present at another conference, teach another course. If graduating debt free is one of your priorities, then perhaps you might choose extra teaching duties over traveling to a conference. But if establishing a network of co-researchers is important, then clearly the conference presentation will net you some contacts. It's not that one choice is de facto better than another. But the pressure to do everything takes its toll, so being strategic in saying "yes" and, especially, "no" is critical.

Richard Ascough,
Queen's University, Religious Studies

The PhD process takes a lot of time out of your life, and a lot of mental energy. It's also designed to build your intellectual resilience. Therefore, I can almost guarantee you will have an existential crisis during your PhD enrolment period, as this process kicks in. You may also have one or more personal life event crises as well – marriages, divorces, babies, ill-health, bereavements, serious adverse weather events, accidents, visa panics – these student issues all routinely pass through my office, and all need attention. If a program is properly designed, it will have some flexibility to allow for humanity to creep in. So, make sure you use this flexibility to make space for the necessary breathing space. That way you will emerge better and stronger, and also be one of the people who finally submits a dissertation. If your program doesn't offer this, move to a better program. Vote with your feet.

Sandra Leaton Gray,
University College London, Education

Flourishing as a PhD student means preparing for your future after graduation even though it may sometimes seem like a distant dream. You want your future to be a healthy mix of a satisfying career and life balance. Lay the groundwork for this now. To help to achieve one part of this goal, document your scholastic and research experience as you go along and communicate your findings. Taking advantage of opportunities to publish, present seminars, and talk with other scholars in your field is most advantageous. Volunteering to do some ad hoc reviews of literature in your field will facilitate critical thinking. Keeping records of these efforts in your curriculum vitae and your teaching dossier is important and asking newly hired professionals, not senior members of faculty, for comment is most worthwhile and relevant. Remember, resumes are important gatekeepers to your future career.

At the same time, set the stage for a balanced and pleasant work and home life, the other crucial part of your future. It can start with little things, exchanging pleasantries with administrative staff, fellow graduates, and faculty, and volunteering with the local high school history or science fair. The ability to be a good listener will help you learn about the support mechanisms, opportunities, and the academic landscape of your country. Most importantly, try to know yourself. Are you creative and productive and more significantly, do you love it? Where do you want to live, in a big city or a small country town? What hobbies, friends, and family are important to you? Do you have medical challenges that must be considered? Relationships are crucial for happiness and deserve investment. What can you do as a partner to foster a relationship? Can you gain satisfaction by contributing to caregiving for loved ones? In all these questions and your answers, be prepared to forgive yourself and to accept with grace the differences in others.

Achieving a perfect equilibrium between work and home life is not effortless and indeed may be difficult to accomplish. It will never be an equal partnership, nor will it remain constant throughout your life. However, thinking about the questions and planning now will help you carve out an exciting, challenging, and satisfying future. Good luck.

Virginia Walker,
Queen's University, Biology

Remember that you are a person with a full life first and foremost. Getting a doctorate is like running a marathon. Rest, good nutrition, social/leisure, and a daily commitment to advance your work is required. Acknowledge that there will be a lot of reading, a lot of writing, and a lot of thinking. Plan for that. Schedule in your time to attend to your physical health, mental health, and get your work done if you need to (especially once the courses are complete and the structure is gone).

Kathryn Hibbert,
Western University, Education

There is no virtue in work per se. Facetime is a scam, and it reproduces harmful forms of bias. Being miserable, working seventy or eighty hours a week – these things have nothing to do with being "serious about your work," they are not sustainable over the long haul, and they will not make your work better as there are severely diminishing returns to exhausted hours of forcing yourself to do things slowly and badly. Learn to organize your time, to set healthy boundaries, and to treat your work as an important part of a healthy life, not an obsession.

Penny Edgell,
University of Minnesota, Sociology

Being a graduate student is not like being an undergraduate; the point is to make a transition from being someone who takes in knowledge – student – to one who produces knowledge – a scholar or a scientist. This transition requires approaching your graduate career as the beginning of your lifelong work, regardless of what you do with your doctorate – if you teach and do research in a university setting or pursue some other path. From day one, make a serious and consistent effort to set yourself up for success over the long haul, from the small things to the big things. On a personal level, you need a secure and happy home environment, supportive relationships, healthy habits, leisure and fun. So, if you haven't already, start taking care of yourself and building a healthy and happy personal life now, instead of waiting "until" (until you finish that preliminary exam or start your dissertation or finish your dissertation or get a job or …).

In terms of your work, this involves mastering two things: being a good professional, and keeping a lively, engaged, relevant intellectual life. Sometimes those pull you in different directions, so learn how to balance your priorities and schedule your time. Learning to teach well, to organize all the information and files for your research projects, to stay on top of email, to communicate professionally, to be visible in your professional societies – those professional skills matter. It also matters to carve out some time each and every week for your own intellectual life. Set aside a weekly time to write in an ideas journal, sharpening your own research questions, working through logical issues in your own analysis or writing, dreaming of projects you may never do. Set aside another chunk of time for research, starting day one; earlier in your program that will be dedicated to reading and taking notes and doing informational coffees and lunches with faculty and more advanced graduate students to learn about their work or resources you can access. Later, it will be time dedicated to your own research and writing, for reading to keep current regarding work relevant to your own research, and the like.

Penny Edgell,
University of Minnesota, Sociology

Avoid isolating yourself as a researcher – research is always collaborative, and you are part of a supportive community of scholars. Avoid isolating yourself socially – the pursuit of perfection is far less important or valuable than a healthy work-life balance. Long hours are often not the most productive. Do not be afraid to value smart working and seizing opportunities to be involved in the broader life of the university and beyond.

Cheryl McEwan,
Durham University, Geography

In these grim times, I can't really write "Don't get discouraged," or "Don't complain." There is a lot that is discouraging and a lot to complain about.

Don't restrict your life entirely to your academic work. Treasure personal relationships; read fiction; go to the theater or concerts; garden; eat good food.

Ann Waltner,
University of Minnesota, History

Learn to put time limits on your work and make space to do something outside of academic life that you're passionate about and engage in this activity on a regular basis. You really need to have something else going on in order to be successful in a PhD program because your brain needs a break, it needs to recharge. Sports, art, music, gardening, birdwatching ... It doesn't matter as long as it gets you away from your coursework, your dissertation, or that article you're trying to get published. Make this activity part of your calendar – it shouldn't be something you only do "if you have the time later" – and set goals for this activity. So, learn to play an instrument better, train for a marathon, or identify ten more species of local birds. Your academic work, and your quality of life more generally, will thank you for finding that other thing you're passionate about.

Rémi A. van Compernolle,
Carnegie Mellon University,
Second Language Acquisition &
French and Francophone Studies

Doing a PhD can be a rather lonely experience, working on an independent project over a period of years, often with quite limited supervision. To minimize the sense of social and intellectual isolation, I encourage students to take as many opportunities as they can to engage with others, try out new ideas and share experiences. Sometimes the most peripheral things can be the most rewarding – working with artists or creative writers, making a podcast, taking part in an exhibition ... Visits to other places are also a good way of thinking outside the box and avoiding a narrow outlook ("We've always done it that way, why would we want to change?"). It's also good to talk to others about the trials and tribulations of being a PhD student – it's very rare to be the only one to be experiencing a particular emotion. Share the joys of intellectual discovery and the breakthrough moments too!

Peter Jackson,
University of Sheffield, Human Geography

Fight against thinking that YOU are your PhD, and that the quality of your writing equates to the worth of you as a person. Anyone who makes any kind of statement to the effect that your work is a proxy of you as a human being deserves to be ignored and disregarded. PhDs are long, and their path is often difficult, rocky, and filled with potholes and byways where emotional and psychological dangers lie in wait to derail and discourage. Not only that, but some academics have ego states that can only be inflated by deflating other people's. And likewise, some doctoral candidate peers have esteem states that can only function when others feel as devastated as they do. Which means that for a lot of doctoral students, paradoxically, supervisors often require you to be at your most resilient when you're actually at your most vulnerable. Recognizing this is one of the very greatest realizations of a student and one of the most subtle skills of a supervisor. In practice, though, for a doctoral candidate, it's exhausting emotional work, but it can be achieved by working on your heart, soul, and body outside of study, by doing things that you enjoy, doing things that you're good at, and most significantly, doing things that show you that although your PhD is a big part of your life, there is most surely life outside of your PhD too.

Caroline Walker-Gleaves,
Newcastle University, Education

Here I will steal the advice of the Nobel Prize–winner Paul Nurse because I think what he has to say on the issue is spot on. His advice is "don't work too hard." There is a gulf between the generation of data and the understanding of data. What I think he means is don't focus on the former at a cost to the latter. The things we don't usually classify as "work" are often more valuable than what looks like work. For me, if I am stuck then I go for a walk or I go for a coffee. Talking about your science over coffee or thinking it through while walking is often a much more productive use of time than generating yet more data. I also find long train journeys are especially conducive to not working too hard. There is a most unhealthy notion that you should be working in a formal sense every waking hour. But as a method to generate insight this seems somewhat lacking and is more a recipe for burnout than for a productive career.

Laurence Hurst,
University of Bath, Evolutionary Genetics

REFLECTION AND APPLICATION ACTIVITIES

The advice in this chapter delves into the challenges of graduate studies. As Kathryn Hibbert suggests, "getting a doctorate is like running a marathon." As a major theme in this book, finding balance is presented as crucial to fulfilling your goals and setting the holistic stage for a life of well-being. As Pamela Rose Toulouse defines it, "balance means that each individual has to have a strategic and purposeful plan on how to be well physically, emotionally, intellectually, and spiritually." Setting boundaries is key – in terms of both limits on the time and energy spent on the PhD work, as well as boundaries on other activities that detract from that work. My Balance Sheet is about your current state. Use this activity to take stock of your situation and mindset and identify potential derailers that are better addressed now. Big Dreams and Small Sparks provides an opportunity for you to connect with your own personal elements of life, both big and small, that bring you joy and contribute to your well-being. Approach this exercise expansively, both to bring self-awareness about your own well-being and as a means to motivate you on a daily basis.

Activity 1: Big Dreams and Small Sparks

What are the big dreams you have for yourself that keep you motivated throughout your PhD and what are the small sparks that ignite your daily work? This activity will help you identify what motivates you so that you keep in balance and steady on your PhD bike.

Small Sparks: Put on a three-minute timer and write down all the things that bring you joy and make you happy. Think about activities, hobbies, actions, and rewards. Don't let your pen stop writing in the three minutes.

Once the three minutes are over, review your list. Identify which items on your list can work as daily motivators to get you started with your work or in achieving your goals. Circle these sparks. This is your list of small sparks. You can add to it as you think of new sparks.

Each morning pick from this list when you are organizing your workday. Be mindful to pick sparks that allow you to seek balance. Emphasize sparks that are relational, social, embodied, and embedded in nature. Let these sparks reward your accomplishments. For example, if you set a goal to write a page of your dissertation, then identify what spark you will give yourself when you achieve it. It is a classic rewards approach, and it works!

Big Dreams: This is the space to think big and dig deep. Why are you doing your PhD and where will it lead you? Again, put on a timer, but this time for fifteen minutes. Once you start the timer, write to the prompt below. Don't stop writing. If you run out of thoughts and "go blank," fill the space with any text that comes to mind.

Prompt: You are ten years older. You are writing a letter to your former self (i.e., who you are right now when reading this book). In your letter, tell your former self where you are in your life ten years later.

- What am I doing for my job?
- What does my life look like?
- What is my family structure?
- What do I spend my time doing?
- What do I want to tell my former self?

Once you have finished, reread what you wrote. Clarify your "big dream" by responding to this question: *Why am I doing my PhD and where will it lead me?* Summarize your response in a few words or a sentence. Answer a second question: *What else do I want my life to be?* Post these two sentences near your workstation. It is essential to realize what we are working toward – both in relation to our doctoral work and in relation to larger life goals.

Activity 2: My Balance Sheet

In this activity, you'll take honest stock of the balance in your current life. First, read the big dreams you outlined in the activity Big Dreams and Small Sparks. Assess the relative importance to you of your PhD in the grand scheme of life and the relative importance of your other big dreams.

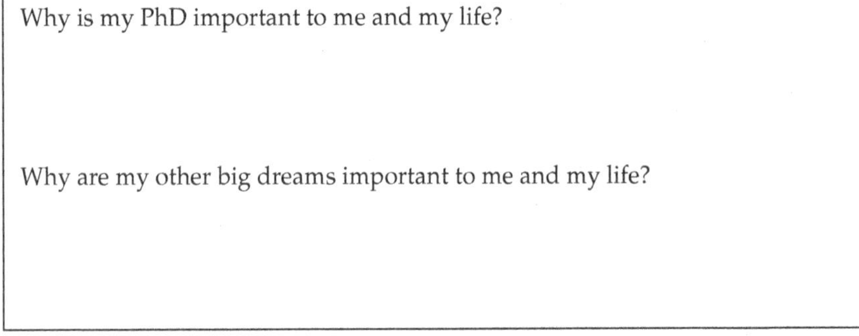
Why is my PhD important to me and my life?

Why are my other big dreams important to me and my life?

In the balance sheet below, list the amount of time and focus you give to your PhD and other aspects of your life over the course of a representative or average week. You might consider:

- Recreational activities
- Socializing with friends
- Family time
- Sleep
- Relaxed meals and meal preparation
- Reading for pleasure
- Exercise

Balance Sheet

Day	PhD-Related Activities	Time (hrs)	Non-PhD-Related Activities	Time (hrs)

Once you've filled in your balance sheet and have an awareness of where and how you focus your time and energy, answer the following questions as honestly as possible.

How well does my Balance Sheet match my PhD dreams?

Not at all 0 1 2 3 4 5 6 7 8 9 10 Perfectly

How well does my Balance Sheet match my big dreams in life?

Not at all 0 1 2 3 4 5 6 7 8 9 10 Perfectly

Activity 3: My Derailers

In taking stock of work-life balance, many of us struggle to fit it all in. Our purposeful plans to be well physically, emotionally, intellectually, and spiritually often get derailed by work and life demands. This activity is designed to help you understand these derailers so you can counteract them.

Area of life out of balance: (exercise, nutrition, sleep, relaxation, social time, writing and thinking time, etc.)	Derailers: Obstacles or life demands preventing me from following through with my plans	Why do these derailers exist? What purpose do they serve? Can they be avoided?

Think of solutions to mitigate each derailer. (e.g., alter schedule, re-prioritize, prepare in the evening for the next day, cut out time-wasters). Address the "why" of your derailers, then make a commitment to alter your habits. Start small; even micro changes can have a powerful impact.

One small change I will make is.....

I will know this change is working when...

Activity 4: The Three Rs of Reflection

Recall: I Must Remember

What are my top takeaways from this chapter?

Revise: What Do I Want to Do Differently?

Based on the advice from this chapter, what is most important for me to personally change or improve? Write down a commitment for one small action you will do differently right away.

Reimagine: What Do I Hope Will Happen?

Reimagining a future reality for ourselves and setting clear intentions is powerful in changing our current practices and achieving our goals. Based on the advice from this chapter, describe a vision of yourself in the future. A prompt for this exercise: *In one year, I hope …*

CHAPTER SIX

Focus on What Matters

It seems that Shiny Ball Syndrome (SBS) – the made-up phenomenon to explain why some people get easily distracted by shiny new things that lead to them abandoning their current task – is on the rise.[1] Perhaps this trend is due to the exponential rate at which new information is generated every second, or the constant state of polycrisis we find ourselves in, or the fact that more people are multitasking across several platforms and devices at any given time. Of the plethora of distractions that tempt us each day and can pull us from our dissertation work, some may be highly valuable pursuits. As Stefan Rinke notes in his advice, the dissertation journey is "a labyrinth of endless possibilities." So how do you choose which paths along the labyrinth are productive possibilities and which are destructive distractions? This chapter provides essential advice to help you tease out the difference and focus on what matters most to you and your goals.

Let's start with productive possibilities. Throughout your studies, unplanned opportunities will surface for you to engage in significant scholarly work. Some of this work will align directly with your dissertation and feed into your PhD studies, whereas some may be more tangential. Nonetheless, when presented with an additional work opportunity, ask yourself these three golden questions:

1. *Does the work align with my PhD or career goals?*
2. *Do I have the time and energy to engage in the work?*
3. *Will the work bring me happiness and satisfaction?*

Three "yeses" are like triple sevens at a slot machine. If you answer yes to all of the questions above, the work will likely be of high reward to you, and you should consider taking it on. Most times, however, you may not have the time to take on the work, though you know it aligns with your PhD goals or brings you happiness. Or you are fearful to take on the work because you aren't confident in your abilities; in the short term you question whether it will bring you happiness despite it being valuable for your long-term career. To navigate these more difficult choices, remember that you can seek support and advice from supervisors and peers, and you can always ask to engage in work on your own terms. For example, perhaps you take on only part of the task, or you ask to do it collaboratively with someone else.

If you are presented with a work opportunity and you respond to the questions above with three "noes" then you should likely not proceed with the opportunity, except for one reason: financial. Due to the current state of graduate-level funding, many PhD students need to take on additional work responsibilities for funding reasons even though these experiences may not directly align with their PhD goals, they may not always have time or energy for these roles, and they may not derive much happiness or satisfaction from them. That said, research assistantships and teaching opportunities do provide valuable contexts to develop important skills applicable to your PhD dissertation and future career. Spending time analyzing and articulating how these experiences connect to your goals can help provide motivation for these positions.

One of the most common reasons that PhD students get overrun with too many projects and work opportunities is that they have not learned how to say "no." While saying "no" may seem like a simple skill, many scholars have struggled to learn it. And this issue is not limited to the academic arena alone. It is recognized as a broader social challenge, so much so that books have been written about the art of saying "no."[2] Our default compulsion to say yes to every request and opportunity is rooted in a broader social desire for inclusion, which manifests through people-pleasing behaviors. In the context of PhD studies, these desires to please others are compounded by job-market fears that push us to take on every opportunity in an effort to maximize our curriculum vitae content for post-PhD employment. Essentially, people-pleasing + FOMO (fear of missing out) = saying yes to everything.

Ironically, when we learn to say no, we have more time to be productive on the tasks that matter, and we become better scholars as a result. In the end, we are more likely to achieve our desired career goals. In his book *The Art of Saying No,* Damon Zahariades states, "saying 'no' to people is one of the most important skills you can develop. It frees you to pursue your own interests, both personal and professional. To that end, it'll boost your productivity, improve your relationships, and fill you with a sense of confident calm that may seem alien to you at this moment."[3] He provides a series of strategies to help you learn how to say "no." The important lesson here is to find a strategy that works for you, one that respects both the person asking for help as well as yourself. We recognize that for PhD students it can be particularly challenging to say "no" to your supervisor. There is an embedded power structure in supervisory relationships, and you may not feel like you are in a position to say "no" to your supervisor's work request. Should you find yourself in this position, most universities have supports for students including peer advisors, graduate chairs, and Associate Deans who can help you negotiate work responsibilities with your supervisor.

There are other kinds of productive possibilities aside from additional work opportunities that may not, at first glance, appear to serve your PhD studies or career prospects, but in fact, do. These possibilities take the form of healthy work-life habits: working out, socializing, spending time in nature, playing games, and family time. Recognizing that well-being is an essential foundation for strong academic work, ensuring time for healthy work-life habits promotes better PhD results. No doubt, you've heard the expression "everything in moderation." Well, counter to common perceptions of PhD life, we advocate for "everything in moderation, including dissertations too." Of course, there will be times when deadlines approach and workloads intensify or when you are on the brink of an exciting discovery and want to document it no matter how long it takes. These moments can be energizing, as much as they can be exhausting. But when you pull back and look at your overall work-life balance, the dissertation should be one aspect of your life and to perform optimally in your dissertation you must take time to smell the proverbial roses. In other words, roses matter too, perhaps much more than we know or give credit to.

So, what about destructive distractions? How do you steer clear of those? There is a point, and sometimes we don't even notice it, much like when we are eating through a bag of potato chips, when a healthy dose of distraction turns into destructive procrastination. A few potato chips are a treat; bag after bag, day after day, is an unhealthy habit. The key is recognizing when a distraction has pulled our focus away from what really matters. There are a number of strategies to help us reflect on this. Here are some of our favorites:

- Meet with your supervisor regularly (i.e., monthly, biweekly) to check in and update on progress and keep that meeting especially if you feel like you haven't made much progress;
- Make a pact with a peer (i.e., an accountability friend) to check in with each other on a weekly basis about progress goals as well as work-life balance;
- Keep daily lists for both dissertation and non-dissertation tasks with a goal to strike a certain number of items from both lists; and finally,

- Recognize that procrastination is part of the process. It can take time to get into a work mindset: that is okay.

Finally, in the category of unpredicted possibilities that definitely matter falls "life." PhDs are long journeys, and several life changes are likely to occur along the way – marriage, children, caring responsibilities, divorce, injury – you name it. All of these things matter. There is a prevailing tendency in the academy to brush life into the margins, like an annotation. Don't settle for this. Your life events should be as front and center as your dissertation because they all contribute to who you are and who you are becoming, scholar and person.

Under the banner of "focusing on what matters," the scholars in this chapter also point to advice about identifying your passions, purpose, and intentions, and letting these guide your decisions – in your dissertation and beyond. In many ways, that is the underlying message of this chapter. It is easy to get distracted by shiny objects but having a clear sense of what you are passionate about and what your goals are (and these might change over time) will help ensure you stay clear of destructive distractions and maximize the many productive possibilities that accompany a PhD.

ADVICE TO FOCUS ON WHAT MATTERS

Successful PhDs know how to take on independent intellectual ownership of their work as a part of the cooperative and collegial scholarly community, and that big idea is critical to learn, live, and own during one's graduate education. A few of the corollary principles from this advice include: (1) Always do your homework – from selecting your program and your advisor, to your project, to your design and methods – you are a small piece of a rich, rich mosaic of past and current work, and it pays off to know what is knowable, from the history of the students who are in the programs you are considering, to the deepest background details of how and why your own project makes sense. Everything at the state of the art represents a controversy; learn all of the stories, weigh the evidence, think clearly about how your work (it's your degree, no one else's) is an actual contribution. (2) Never forget that your only goal in a graduate program is to get out of it – investigate the background broadly, see where your work fits in, and explore weird areas outside of your own that might make analogical contributions; but in the end, figure out how to define clearly the boundaries of a dissertation rather than try to define a career. Avoid mission creep in your project; you will never answer every question, nor create the work that is equivalent to a lifetime's effort. In the end, graduate school IS school, after all. Get out. You are responsible for making the argument for your own graduation. (3) Proofreading your own ideas is more difficult than proofreading your writing – so build and embrace (internal) reflective critique along with the value that comes from having (external) smart people who will review and engage you with open, candid feedback that you shut up and listen to. (4) Live up to your potential because the "bar" of excellence is not absolute, but a sliding scale – your advisors, your peers, and your colleagues are constantly trying to figure out where your potential is to be able to set an expectation for your achievement. Do not look to someone who did the minimum to get your inspiration; just the opposite.

Brian P. Coppola,
University of Michigan, Chemistry

One of the most common mistakes doctoral students make is collecting too much data! Students often use only half of their data. They spend so much time collecting data they lose precious time for writing and when faced with the mounds of data collected the analysis is overwhelming. Often students collect enough data for three theses. To overcome this problem, they must (with the supervisor's assistance):

- Make sure their questions are not too broad;
- Make sure there are not too many questions;
- Make sure they do not have too many data collection points.

Often students want to collect survey data and do interviews and focus groups. This is too much because they have to design the instruments, learn how to analyze different forms of data, and then connect the data. Just doing well-structured, focused interviews will provide all of the information they need. Piloting the instruments will help ensure they will gather quality data and estimate the quantity of data they collect (then they can adjust). Don't drown in data and remember that trying to write about a massive amount of data is daunting and difficult. Leave some of the data collection until you are doing a postdoctoral fellowship or for your first academic position. Your thesis is a stepping-stone to your next job. You do not have to do it all in one thesis.

Clare Kosnik,
University of Toronto, Education

PhD students sometimes absorb the idea that the most important thing they can do is publish, and that they should get down to it as soon as possible. Fellowships, postdocs, and success on the job market all seem to hinge on a record of publications. But publishing is only part of the story, because to publish well, you have to have something to say, and almost nobody arrives in a doctoral program having great things to say. Classes and qualifying exams are not just annoying obstacles that hinder your pathway to publication: you really do need to learn your field inside and out before you are able to make a useful contribution, because you do not know what a contribution is until you have marinated in how smart people in the past have thought about it. Imagine a world in which everyone who has taken a class or two on statistics thinks that they are thereby able to issue pronouncements on, say, the epidemiology of pandemics. Worse still, imagine that they, rather than trained experts in public health, were able to guide government policy. We don't want to live in that world. Become an expert, then publish.

Jerry Davis,
University of Michigan,
Management and Organizations

Avoid getting caught up in department politics or graduate student–centered policy fights. This is a lemma to the above; you only have so much time to create a portfolio of work and skills that will carry you forward for the rest of your time and career. Don't waste that time on things that are only of concern at a particular institution or for that short period of time. Focus on writing, research, and engaging in the intellectual exchanges of your discipline. So talks and seminars are worth the time invested because they give you ideas and keep you current.

James Moody,
Duke University, Sociology

Be curious! In the early stages of your PhD studies, your supervisor may have assigned you a research topic. But don't expect your supervisor to come up with all the research ideas for your thesis. Read the current literature; follow the news and discuss your research with your fellow graduate students and other interested parties. Remember that once you receive your PhD and start working as an academic, it is up to you to generate new ideas for your research. Learn how to work as an independent researcher.

Make sure that what you are doing is (i) original, (ii) interesting, (iii) technically correct, and (iv) well-written. There is so much competition these days that any manuscript that doesn't satisfy one of these requirements will be quickly rejected. Remember, in our business, it is "Publish or Perish"!

If your research involves mathematical modelling (as in my field of operations research/management science), make sure that you start with a small-scale version, understand how it behaves, and then gradually make your model more realistic. This is known as "sneaking up on the problem."

If you find an academic position after your PhD, you will have to teach courses. For people who don't like it, teaching can be painful. So, try to enjoy teaching, learn from the best practices you have observed from your own professors, and have fun in class. To practice this, try to teach a course or two during your time as a PhD student. You may be working in a university for the next forty-plus years (which is my case); make the best of it and follow the maxim "Do what you love; and love what you do."

If English is your second language, you have more work to do. Don't limit your reading to academic papers and books. Read magazines, newspapers, and novels and stories written by the best writers of the English language. My favorite writer is Somerset Maugham and I have read everything he has written, and everything written about him. It's exciting to be an amateur expert in something other than your academic discipline.

But above all, in your dealings with your friends, colleagues, and future students and everyone else, follow the Golden Rule and be kind.

Mahmut Parlar,
McMaster University, Operations Management

There needs to be a balance between process and thinking strategically for your future. By process, I mean noting those key items that you pick up along the way. This could be found in the ways that your identity intersects with certain methodologies. It could be how you and your identity are taken up in specific spaces. Always take notes, not classroom notes, but notes of your processes around learning and research – this will help you with critical insights, reflexivity, and how you want to take space as an academic. In terms of looking to the future, PhD students must strategically use their learning time to prepare them for being academics, researchers, and professors. Keep relevant, ensure that your work is reflective of what is required in your field so you can be in service to future learners. Perhaps most importantly, always hold space for others – your fellow learners and the students who you in turn will teach.

Mirna Carranza,
McMaster University, Social Work

In the 2000s a typical long German word emerged among young hipsters: Lebensabschnittspartnerschaft. Basically, it means that in the new millennium human relationships are not meant for a lifetime anymore but only for a part of a life. While this is not my concept on a personal level, I tell my PhD students that they should consider their project as a Lebensabschnittspartnerschaft. They should fall in love with it passionately and miss it every second they are without it. When the initial enthusiasm subsides, they should work on their relationship with perseverance and patience to rekindle the fire. Most importantly, they should not forget that the moment will come when this partnership will be ending. The longer the partnership has lasted, the harder it can be to say goodbye, therefore: stick to the essentials, i.e., your thread and your central question.

Stefan Rinke,
Freie Universität Berlin, Latin American History

There are lots of good reasons for embarking on a PhD program – the thrill of discovering a new insight; fieldwork in exotic places; intellectual discourse; personal growth in self-motivation and project management; or simply as a means to improve your career opportunities. But the journey is challenging, and I would encourage you to not avoid reminding yourself and your significant family and friends what motivated you to start in the first place. This can garner personal resilience in the face of intellectual and logistical challenges (or even the sheer boredom of inevitably repetitive research activities). It can also offer a useful perspective, if those motivations change or elements of the journey are affecting your health and well-being. The personal costs of undertaking a PhD shouldn't be underestimated, but it is your journey so don't forget to keep it fun – or reflect honestly if it ceases to be.

Mark Elgar,
University of Melbourne, BioSciences

It's very important to be curious, but you should avoid exploring every new avenue for your research as that can be counterproductive. Be very selective about the projects you spend your time on (make sure you discuss your ideas very thoroughly with your supervisor, advisory committee, and peers), as the time to do bench research will go by very fast, and a ten-year PhD is not a good thing to list on your CV!

Emma Allen-Vercoe,
University of Guelph, Molecular and Cellular Biology

"It's never too early to be happy!" or, in this context, it's never too early to work on a/several research project(s) that you care about. Yes, getting a glowing reference letter from your supervisor is important, but it should not mean sacrificing your interests and passion to work on a project that you don't necessarily "connect to." For one, during your PhD, hard times (and there inevitably are some …) will be easier to overcome when working on research that is dear to your heart. Second, you will be more creative and eager to learn more on a subject that you feel is "part of you." Finally, in many job applications, you'll be judged by your engagement, thoroughness, dedication, and enthusiasm, and what better way to "sell yourself" than to talk about things that you have loved doing?

Anne Petitjean,
Queen's University, Chemistry

Avoid becoming an unquestioning member of your research community. Your job is to become an expert in the specific focus of your research, but not to stop asking questions. Keep your focus on your research purpose and question whenever you have doubts. You need to become a member of your research community and contribute your new knowledge from your PhD work. But avoid becoming an unquestioning disciple and remember that you are valued for your contributions, which include questioning and bringing new ideas. A research community is a kind of mutual admiration society, so be clear about its purpose, your purpose, and your role in the community. At the same time be aware of the "rules of power" (e.g., *The 48 Laws of Power*, by Robert Greene); support your colleagues, don't embarrass them, help look after your supervisor, yet question when you should.

Bruce MacDonald,
University of Auckland, Engineering

A doctorate is an adventure that leads to unexpected and unforeseen paths, which can occasionally be surprising and destabilizing. Committing oneself to a doctorate supposes a fair amount of curiosity, ambition, as well as a desire for freedom of thought and action. Many paths will present themselves and you will have to choose one or another research track, which might very well shape your life. It is important not to lose sight of THE problem you have formulated, the goals you have set, and your aspirations; it is a question of balance. The different paths can enrich your work and help you deepen your understanding, but they can also make you lose sight of the problem you identified, the objectives you selected, and your professional goals. You will strike a balance between the potential and the possible by making periodic adjustments, and this will give nuance to your openness to new ideas by the demonstration of your convictions reinforced in the course of your research. Where several paths intersect, one can either go astray or gain much from discoveries found while wandering momentarily; consider the story of Little Thumbling who found his way back home by marking his passage with clever clues. Be methodical, reflective, determined, and keep at hand your compass in order to consolidate your position as a researcher capable of discerning that which is pertinent to the resolution of the problem and that which deviates from it. The initial question that started your work springs from a personal process, an impulse that drives you to want to contribute to the ongoing construction of knowledge. Stoke the fire and, as the French writer Nicolas Boileau advises, "Put your work twenty times upon the anvil."

Jocelyne Mathieu,
Université Laval, Historical Sciences

Doing a PhD is a full-time job! And it consists of simultaneously doing both your doctoral research and laying the foundation of your academic career. You must commit entirely to working on your research, building your publication file, and establishing your network of collaborators. Carefully plan out your work schedule. Make the most of every opportunity (to contribute to research projects, write articles, present at conferences, or give talks) that is presented to you … and create other opportunities. Your first ally in achieving this should be your doctoral supervisor. Therefore, make sure that you choose them wisely prior to joining a doctoral program. Meet with them. Inquire about the resources they can provide you to help you complete your PhD. And present them with opportunities to collaborate. Every collaboration you will share with them is an occasion to develop your professional knowledge. Your mentor will guide you, introduce you to research projects, to academic publishing, to knowledge transfer, to collaborators and colleagues. You will gain from each of them, and so will your supervisor. Be fully engaged in your doctoral project. And always try to have some fun doing it.

Thierry Giasson,
Université Laval, Journalism

Avoid losing sight of what it is that you are really up to. The thesis is a process, and although it is, for most of us, the highest qualification we will achieve, it is still, for all that, an examination. Or to put it another way, it is only a thesis. Avoid trying to compose something that you can't; remember that this is a thesis for examination. It is not a monograph. And, even if it contains pieces that you have published elsewhere, you are bringing it together for the purposes of examination and to persuade the examiners of its merits. A doctoral thesis is required to do two things: show your knowledge of the field; and make an original contribution to the field. Rather than get strung up on originality, think of it like this – anyone (including an examiner) can read the available sources and literature. What will your work show them that they can't get otherwise? And when you get corrections at your viva or defense – just make the corrections you are asked to. It's only a thesis. The book comes later.

Giles Gasper,
Durham University, High Medieval History

Avoid the temptation to apply for every grant, to submit to every conference, or to sign up for every workshop that happens to show up in your inbox. Many of these things will end up being distractions for you – more is not always better, and that includes the lines on your CV. Your time is valuable, and you need to set limits, so stay away from anything that does not advance your research in a meaningful way, bring you closer to completion of the PhD, or contribute significantly and concretely to your teaching and professional development.

Rémi A. van Compernolle,
Carnegie Mellon University,
Second Language Acquisition &
French and Francophone Studies

Avoid the rush to publish. Importantly, this advice isn't saying that you shouldn't publish as a graduate student – for better or worse, landing a job these days requires (multiple) publications. Rather, the advice here counsels a combination of restraint and encouragement.

The need for restraint is twofold. First, writing for journals is different than writing seminar papers or dissertation chapters – they're almost different genres. So success demands developing an eye for what a truly novel contribution to the literature is and avoiding the pitfall of submitting something that will only be deemed "too graduate student-y" by editors and reviewers. Second, getting a paper published is hard. Most top journals have single-digit acceptance rates – many very good papers get rejected. So before you submit, take the time to make sure your paper is solid.

The encouragement is this. Graduate school offers you something rare: the time to think big. You shouldn't waste that opportunity. As you work on your dissertation, you are working on a project that will provide the foundation for much that you do as an assistant professor on the tenure clock. So while it's important to publish as a grad student, it's also important to take advantage of the freedom that you have to think about what kind of researcher you want to be, and how to get there from where you are.

Charlie Kurth,
Clemson University, Philosophy

So you've made it, you've been accepted into a PhD program. What's more, the university community acknowledges your many talents. you have writing skills, you quickly grasp the issues at play in a field, you can capture the students' attention, you are particularly gifted at developing argumentative texts and analyzing data, and you are like a fish in water when it comes to coordinating the activities of a research group. Once people become aware of your skills, it is highly likely that you will receive numerous proposals for work and collaboration. Are all these proposals good opportunities for your PhD trajectory and career path? No. Can a PhD student afford to refuse proposals from the very same university community that might eventually hire him or her once the PhD has been obtained? Yes. When doing a PhD, you have to set goals and determine the means needed to attain them. Generally, two aspects need to be planned: one, your PhD trajectory, and two, enhancing your résumé in order to be in a good position for postdoctoral work, a research position, or a teaching job once you have successfully defended your PhD thesis. This planning means you have to prioritize certain activities, which also means refusing proposals that are obviously interesting but that will take you too far away from your ultimate goals. I often compare these opportunities to a train that pulls into a station. You can't take all the trains, you can't go in all directions, because you risk never submitting your thesis. As the old saying goes, "A good thesis is a finished thesis."

Marie-Christine Saint-Jacques,
Université Laval,
Family Transitions and Child Protection Law

"Think deeply about simple things," which is a sage motto that appears to be attributed to the mathematician C. Gauss. Test your new ideas against known results, and ask yourself "What is being gained?" and "Is what results 'too good to be true?" etc. Be curious. Experiment with new ways of achieving old results. Too often, it feels like students are attempting to tackle difficult problems by mimicry rather than establishing a thorough understanding of their machinery.

Embrace teaching! Giving deep thought to the relatively elementary topics within your field allows you to have an impact and share intuition and inspiration. Being receptive to the thought processes of your students will deepen your own understanding. An extension of this to research topics is also valuable. By practicing explaining their arguments to non-experts, budding researchers will learn to identify the key innovation and to make analogies that can have long-term benefits.

Jason Metcalfe,
University of North Carolina at Chapel Hill, Mathematics

Be willing to explore, and then reflect. Doctoral training is premised on specialization. Many doctoral students come into graduate school already committed to a specific research project rather than a broad intellectual agenda. Most doctoral advisers also emphasize the need for students to narrow their focus and then burrow into a well-defined problem. That approach will always be a key element of graduate school. But it should not come at the expense of engagement with cognate disciplines, exposure to collaborative projects, and cultivation of versatile communication skills – the ability to convey complex ideas clearly to peers, to academics in other fields, to broader publics (including students!), and to decision-makers. Such endeavors allow doctoral students to build wider intellectual networks, find multiple mentors, and gain confidence. And if they are accompanied by periodic reflection, PhD students tend to identify their intellectual priorities and passions more effectively; they also get a better handle on career aspirations, whether those aspirations have an academic or non-academic trajectory.

Edward Balleisen,
Duke University, History and Public Policy

Throughout my career, I have benefited from the advice of several teachers and mentors. The ones that I enjoyed the most were the ones who did not give me all the answers, but made me think outside of the box and made me look at both sides of every reality. The single most important piece of advice PhD students need to heed in order to thrive in their doctoral program is to own their project from the beginning. They will spend several years of their life working on their research project and this project will be a determining element for their future life, whatever career they decide. They should not be just doing the experiments. They should learn, experiment, then read, think, and plan, and experiment again. A PhD is a process useful for the whole life, providing a unique opportunity to learn not to give up at the first obstacles, but push through the unknown, imagine the best solutions, and flourish as a critical mind.

Pia Wintermark,
McGill University, Pediatrics

The behaviors that I like to see and encourage in PhD students are (1) critical thinking – really this is the hallmark of a great PhD student and academic in general. The ability to critique ideas and theory will help you to push the boundaries of your discipline area; (2) openness to ideas, to opportunities, to collaborations, to different perspectives; (3) collegiality and generosity of spirit and a recognition that we are all in this big endeavor together and that giving of oneself is important in academia. Trust me, you will be rewarded in-kind; and (4) resilience and the strength of character to ride through the rough patches while keeping a firm eye on the end goal – completion of the PhD!

Mark Bellgrove,
Monash University, Cognitive Neuroscience

Theory is your friend. As well as the other friends you can make through your PhD – your supervisors, other PhD students, and new networks in industry – theory will help get you through some rocky ground. A good theory helps you explain your data, giving you language and concepts to turn your facts into principles and possibilities. A rich theory helps you understand yourself, challenges the way you see the world, and starts to leak into your everyday life to help you solve problems in new ways. A useful theory helps you create clever diagrams that encapsulate your findings in a way that is shareable, memorable, and clear. So take your time to explore a few different theoretical perspectives during your PhD, trying them on for size. That is not a sidetrack or a waste of time. When you explore and play with theories you are sharpening your concepts and ways of thinking, exactly what you should be doing in a PhD. You will know when you find a theory that brings you joy and the pieces of your research puzzle all seem to click into place. You can turn to the theory to think about that puzzle piece that just isn't coming into focus. And like a friend, the right theory can reassure you that you are doing fine.

Jill Willis,
Queensland University of Technology, Education

Understand purpose in all your work, high level to low level and start to end. Firstly, continually remind yourself of the purpose of your research. How will it make the world a better place, how will it help people, and keep your effort aligned with the purpose. Keep focused on this purpose, use it to avoid being distracted or sidetracked. Choose a supervisor you connect with, and who also has a purpose aligned with your research purpose, or the other way around, choose a supervisor who aligns with your values and then a research topic that aligns with your supervisor's purpose. Secondly, focus on the purpose of your research decisions. When you talk and write about your research, be sure to explain why you chose each method, design, and parameter. Thirdly, understand the purpose of research and science; read Karl Popper's *Conjectures and Refutations* about the modern scientific method (it's available online). Become an expert on your research purpose; read widely and broadly about it, go to conferences clearly focused on the purpose, get to know the key people who also focus on this purpose. Get to know the local researchers who are related to your purpose and work together with them to follow your purpose.

Bruce MacDonald,
University of Auckland, Engineering

A PhD is not a vocational degree. You should strategize all the way through your degree so that you emerge well-prepared into a job market with both academic and non-academic possibilities. But if you see a doctorate primarily as a way to get a job, you are in the wrong place. Leave now, before it grinds you down. There are much better ways you can spend four to six years if your goal is a job at the other end. A PhD is a process of personal fulfillment by contributing meaningfully to the human project, to the way we understand each other and our place in the universe. It's a calling. A dissertation should be an act of love. If you're here out of love, you're in the right place. Live the dream!

Randy Allen Harris,
University of Waterloo,
Linguistics, Rhetoric,
and Communication Design

On finding such a problem for research, I would advise the student to think independently and NOT read up on all that has been done on the topic. If one is always reading the literature, one would never get started. After a period of independent thought, say about four months, the student can cautiously read on what has been done in a very selective manner and compare their approach with past attempts and progress. Invariably, there will be a new idea in the independent thought. At least this has been my experience for almost forty years of research.

Ram Murty,
Queen's University, Mathematics

Avoiding an all or nothing approach is helpful. Living, eating, and breathing the PhD doesn't allow for downtime – a reflective space – which is often when important insights ("aha" moments) appear. Also, most problems can be overcome with good support and supervision so don't avoid speaking to your supervisors about personal and academic problems. Changes in methodology and even topic, while seemingly daunting, can occur and are usually for the best in the long run. Some supervisors will advise students to go away and read for lengthy periods, particularly at the start, but the PhD process does need structure, so reading without a purpose may not be the best advice and guided reading with some idea of the PhD structure will provide a useful sense of direction and reassurance about what matters.

In addition, try not to avoid friends, family, pets, and your own health and well-being – the PhD process can be an isolating one and participating in the "real world" provides a welcome change and relief. Do try and avoid binaried or black-and-white thinking – being open to multiple perspectives is interesting and useful. Also avoid being too serious and try and find the fun and humor to help sustain you on your journey. One way to do this might be to use metaphors such as swimming without floaties, planting and nurturing seeds, and (when you are in the final tiring stages but that blissful end is in sight) that a PhD is like running a marathon and you are entering the stadium for the last charge home! Also avoid not attending your graduation. You deserve to wear that floppy hat and for your family and friends to be there to "yahoo" and congratulate you on this amazing achievement – it is your portable ticket that no one can take away from you!

Margaret Simmons,
Monash University, Medicine

From my perspective, being pulled in too many directions is something that doctoral students need to resist. It is so easy to become swept up with the many activities surrounding research activity and being a research student. Such a variety of activities too – from workshops about the research process, to courses on skill development, to contributions to forums, to departmental seminars, to research student meetings and events to attend or even organize.

All of these activities do have their merits, so I am certainly not saying they are to be avoided completely. However, being strategic about where to put one's energies is highly important. That is not to say that there is no room for engaging in activities that are nice to be involved in or simply because they are interesting, but staying true to the overall goal of achieving a great doctoral outcome is paramount.

Having been a primary supervisor on a number of occasions for doctoral researchers who are studying part-time and by distance has emphasized to me just how important it is for doctoral researchers to stay focused. Family, work, and community are full-time parts of anyone's life and integrating all of that with formal research and study work is quite the challenge. Motivation, energy, and capacity can often come under threat when someone is undertaking a candidature that can last for six years plus! A strong support network from home, work, colleagues, as well as university, is essential. Family and work have to, and inevitably will, be priorities for doctoral students, so having a plan for the candidature that incorporates elements of flexibility as the norm will build in capacity for the student to step back from the intensity of the research work for short periods to take holidays, and deal with unexpected events and the like when needed.

Sarah Stein,
University of Otago, Education

"This is only a doctoral degree." When you are in the trenches of your degree it is hard to keep things in perspective, especially when things are not going well. Students make a lot of sacrifices to undertake their doctoral studies and it is easy to lose sight of things that are important, such as well-being and downtime. Three things may help students with this: 1) With all students that I supervise we make time early in the supervision to talk about their priorities both within their studies and outside. This helps me to get to know them as individuals and to understand their motivations, and it helps them to clarify their expectations. I encourage students to take the lead in having these conversations with their supervisors. 2) At the start of each supervision meeting my supervisees and I touch base about life – family, pets, interests, challenges – before launching into discussions about the topic at hand. I think it is realistic for students to expect a level of empathy and understanding from their supervisors about how they are coping. As I am one of the people that they have the most contact with during their studies I feel that I have a duty of care to help my supervisees to manage their expectations and keep things in perspective. That said, you can't take their problems on yourself. They are adults and need the space to be responsible, but a guiding hand does not go amiss. Be confident to ask for help when you need it. 3) Administrative and professional staff are the glue of every department. Cultivate your administrators. They know the systems and the people to ask. If something goes wrong, they can invariably find a way to fix it. You don't need to give them flowers and chocolates every week, although I'm sure it will be appreciated.

Sarah Carr,
University of Otago, Business

REFLECTION AND APPLICATION ACTIVITIES

The advice in this chapter provides a wide range of perspectives on what is important for the PhD journey, where to focus, and where not to focus. You'll see overlap in these ideas, as these excellent supervisors recommend fostering relationships and seeking balance as important goals! Others talk about the importance of thinking and curiosity, connecting with your intellectual purpose and maintaining that connection in the bigger context of your life and career. Focus on Goals and Passions provides an opportunity to connect with the harbor on your horizon, the desired destination of your personal PhD journey, to help decide what's most important to you.

Advice in this chapter expresses ideas about the benefits of saying "yes," as well as emphasizing the importance of cultivating the skill of saying "no." Distracting Decisions presents an opportunity to reflect on your own patterns in what you decide to say "yes" and "no" to. Consider whether you're leaning too far one way or another, in light of your long-term goals.

Activity 1: Focus on Goals and Passions

Focusing on what matters requires being clear about your goals and passions. Complete the table below to identify your goals and passions related to your dissertation, career, and life (family, friends, hobbies, financial, etc.). You can interpret the life category broadly and expand it as needed. Keep in mind that your goal is what you hope to achieve. For this activity, we are asking you to identify a three-, five-, and ten-year goal. Your passion is the underlying, driving force that keeps you interested in your goal.

Goals & Passion	Career	PhD Studies & Dissertation	Life (expand as needed)
Three-Year Goal			
Five-Year Goal			
Ten-Year Goal			
My Passion			

Activity 2: Distracting Decisions

Reflect back on a recent decision you had to make about doing something for someone else or taking on additional work. Think about the decision you ended up making. Now, ask yourself these three questions in relation to the decision:

a. Did the work align with my goals (PhD, career, personal)?
b. Did I have the time and energy to engage the work or take on the task?
c. Did the work bring me happiness and satisfaction?

Repeat this process with three to five decisions you have made in the past and see if you notice any patterns about your decision-making process. Take note of these patterns as you are faced with decisions in the future.

Activity 3: The Three Rs of Reflection

Recall: I Must Remember

What are my top takeaways from this chapter?

Revise: What Do I Want to Do Differently?

Based on the advice from this chapter, what is most important for me to personally change or improve? Write down a commitment for one small action you will do differently right away.

Reimagine: What Do I Hope Will Happen?

Reimagining a future reality for ourselves and setting clear intentions is powerful in changing our current practices and achieving our goals. Based on the advice from this chapter, describe a vision of yourself in the future. A prompt for this exercise: *In one year, I hope …*

CHAPTER SEVEN

Cultivate a Growth Mindset

Everybody fails. *Everybody*. You might even say that success is impossible without failure, because if you're seeking, attempting, striving, failure is inevitable, at least sometimes. As Albert Einstein said, "You never fail until you stop trying." Is this how the academy defines failure? As something inevitable or even positive? By the time a PhD student enters their program, their success to date has been determined by high grades, which control access to opportunity. Failure in a graduate student's research comes about when ideas or methods are rejected, or writing does not meet standards or conventions. These failures are tangible, with real consequences for graduate students' lives, livelihoods, and sense of worth.

Whether high stakes or low stakes, "failure is an important part of your growth," as Michelle Obama puts it. It's not whether you fail – we all do – it's how you handle it that counts. Of course, it's natural to have negative emotions surrounding failure, recognizing that the word holds different meanings for people. We define failure as *a situation when a desired outcome or result does not happen*. By this definition, failure is unique, based on each individual's desired outcomes.

In an academic environment, in addition to all the closed doors and potential career implications, there's a substantial social component to failure. You, as a PhD student, are surrounded by others who achieve the outcomes that you desire, get the positions you want, fall easily (it seems!) into postdocs, grants, and faculty positions, and have their articles accepted by top journals. Immediate comparison between your own failure and someone else's success can affect your perception of self – your identity – as well as how others perceive you. In academic circles, your achievements influence your social standing and your sense of belonging. These realities take a substantial toll on mental health and likely contribute to the mental health crisis among graduate students.[1] While any career path is littered with setbacks, failure in the crucible of academia may have more prominent effects, with substantial, far-reaching psychological and life-course consequences. These considerations make handling the inevitable setbacks that come with being a doctoral student even *more* important. Fortunately, moving forward positively from any "size" or "stake" of failure is possible when you nurture a growth mindset.

Focusing on growth is not some trite or frivolous concept; it's an empirically researched success strategy. Indeed, a growth mindset[2] has been shown to impact academic success,[3] motivation,[4] and well-being.[5] Carol Dweck[6] describes mindset as the self-conceptions that "people use to structure the self and guide their behavior." A growth mindset is a deep-seated belief that intelligence, personality, and character "are not simply a hand you're dealt and have to live with, always trying to convince yourself and others that you have a royal flush when you're secretly worried it's a pair of tens." Instead, a growth mindset is the belief that "your basic qualities are things you can cultivate through your efforts."

To define a growth mindset, it is useful to distinguish it from a fixed mindset.

Fixed Mindset	Growth Mindset
Gives up easily	Persists when faced with setbacks
Avoids challenges	Embraces challenges
Sees effort as fruitless: you are or you aren't, you can or you cannot	Sees effort as the way to develop competence and ultimately mastery
Ignores or avoids negative feedback as it is about the self	Embraces criticism as a means to learn
Others' success is a threat, and a confirmation of one's lesser ability	Others' success is a result of their effort and learning, and so a source of inspiration as well as lessons to apply to one's own life

Someone with a strong growth mindset still feels the sting of failure, but it doesn't define them; it does not signify that they, themselves, are a failure. Instead, failures are challenges "to be faced, dealt with, and learned from." A growth mindset is associated with resilience, as well as ultimately superior outcomes! It turns out that with a growth mindset, you do grow, and continue to grow, and reap the achievements that come with that growth.

If you are right now beginning to worry about whether your own mindset is growth-oriented enough, it's time to start practicing cultivating growth! Because research has demonstrated quite convincingly that a growth mindset can be nurtured. Carol Dweck suggests praising children for their efforts, their strategies, and their improvement to help cultivate their growth. She espouses giving children the message that they are not YET able to do a task, rather than simply not able to do a task. In this case, what's good for the child is good for the adult; we can all give ourselves these strong messages as we face our trials and tribulations. In our own self-talk, we shall replace the words "I can't do this" with "I can't do this YET." For example, "It's not that I can't give a world-class research presentation, it's that I have not yet put in the time and effort to master this skill."

Carol Dweck and others[7] have improved growth mindset in education settings by teaching students that learning something new and difficult causes the brain to form new, stronger connections that over time make a person "smarter." The findings are quite clear – a growth mindset can be taught, and even short information sessions have been found to produce significant effects that last. The metaphor of the brain as a muscle that develops with practice has been a useful means of influencing mindset. You can apply these intervention strategies to your own mindset. You can adjust your self-talk, educate yourself about a growth mindset and its influence on well-being and achievement, and remind yourself of the power of mindset in times of setbacks, just when you need it most.

In addition to internalizing the idea that ability develops with effort, there are further mental "tricks" you can try that research[8] suggests may be of benefit. For one, you can visualize the change that is going to happen, even as you experience failure; imagine yourself mastering the skills in question, and the success that comes with it. You might also teach others – students or peers – about growth mindset; one intervention had participants write encouraging letters to others about growth mindset. Not only will you be reinforcing the concepts for yourself, but you'll also be making a difference to others. One intriguing result from a national experiment in an education setting[9] suggests that messages of growth from a group of peers impacts achievement. In other words, cultivating a growth mindset *culture* reinforces the belief system and its positive benefits for all.

The advice that follows may not reference a growth mindset directly, but you'll see shades of it. If you read closely, you might even notice evidence of a growth mindset among these successful faculty! While a growth mindset may not prevent failure, it will soothe the sting and provide fuel to propel you forward.

ADVICE FOR FOCUSING ON GROWTH

One of the most important pieces of information I make sure to transmit to my PhD students concerns the length of doctoral studies and their repercussions on their determination: it is essential for all students to know that there will be ups and downs during their research and writing phases. This is to be expected: the thrill of being admitted to a new program, the eagerness to start their research, and the joy of obtaining funds for their expenses will be matched by the fatigue of a multi-year learning and experimenting process, the fear of failing, the possible repeated failures to produce expected results, the spectrum of the white page, and by the vicissitudes of life that can extend the time of their studies.

These situations have been plaguing generation after generation of PhD students. They are part of the self-discovery process and they are also a screening test: if students can rise above these hurdles and see them for what they truly are, temporary obstacles, then they will succeed.

I also tell my students that part of a supervisor's role is to give them the mental tools to flourish, and to share with them stories of success.

Philippe Caignon,
Concordia University, French Studies

I remember Mrs. Henry from middle school French class, Mr. Gus from high school history class, and Mrs. Schneider who was so very excited to be in the classroom with us. They influenced me greatly and I knew I wanted to teach and was trained as an undergrad for grades seven to twelve. And even though my mentor teacher was great (thirty-seven years ago!), I knew that I did not want to deal with students in grades seven to twelve, or their parents, chaperone school dances and football games, or have cafeteria duty. Gotta love people who work in K–12 schools, but it wasn't for me. So, I had to get a PhD.

I got married weeks before beginning my graduate program at UPenn. We moved to Philadelphia, got familiar with the city, looked for jobs for my husband, and learned to say "hoagies" instead of "subs." That was the least of my culture shock, however, once the program began in earnest. I quickly realized that, although I hadn't known the term at the time, I suffered from imposter syndrome. You've experienced it – questioning why you began a PhD especially since you were waitlisted in the first place, debating why you didn't just decide to simply get a "real job" and save enough money to buy a house with a white picket fence in New Jersey and start having babies (because your younger brothers all had jobs and houses), and asking what in the name of all that is good on the Earth are they talking about in the literary theory courses??

Graduate school is about pride and determination. You got in – it doesn't matter if you were on the bottom of the admissions list or even waitlisted; you go to class – even if you haven't finished the reading; you do your homework – even if you don't fully understand it; you teach the undergrads assigned to you – even if they didn't do their homework; and you begin to make your path forward. You stay the course, trudge along, steer the ship – although there are hurricanes and storms along the way, lots of crying probably, and money problems. You wonder when you'll get a job – "Yes, mom, grandpa, friend A, and brother B, I will eventually have independent income" – and when the anxiety will end – don't get less than a B!! comps?? dissertation??

If you think about something that you've conquered in your life that was difficult, remember that this too shall pass. It may seem like a lifetime (it took me seven years and threats of nulling my coursework), but there is a light at the end of the tunnel and the knowledge that once you finish your PhD, people will have to call you "Doctor" (it's great, even if your kids tell you that you aren't a "real" doctor).

The job question is separate. But I've been reading about Millennials and Gen X and Gen Z – you have many more opportunities than my generation did. Don't believe me? I've had ONE job since I graduated from UPenn. Granted, I love it, enjoy my work, get along with my colleagues (mostly), and am independent in my teaching and research. But you, you don't have to follow the same path that my generation did. You don't have to go into teaching and research – you can work in any field that will have you, in a job that makes you smile. It won't be easy to get a job, it never is. But when you find your path, you'll smile (most of the time). The thing about paths, though, is that they're never truly straight and there are a lot of trees in the way, so don't fret.

And yes, I love metaphors.

Bonnie L. Youngs,
Carnegie Mellon University,
French and Francophone Studies

Intellectual arrogance is to be avoided at all costs. Once you start to believe that you no longer need to pay attention to ideas that are beneath you, you will stop learning. Complacency is the antithesis of discovery. Avoid believing that you cannot learn something new from something – you are just not being creative enough. To learn to execute well, you must constantly be learning from others, listening, and adapting.

Becoming extremely knowledgeable in your subject will make you an expert in your field. Remember to keep the outside world in perspective. Try to purposefully humble yourself occasionally, in different situations and contexts. Try to understand why you believe that an idea is not worth your time. Never stop learning.

Brian Chen,
McGill University, Neuroscience

Patience. Be patient with yourself. Understand that you do not enter a doctoral program with a mastery of the subject and the techniques: that's why you're a PhD student! It will take time to gain the requisite skills, along with the judgment and experience needed to produce good research. Don't benchmark yourself against others who came in with different skill sets and levels of experience – this is self-defeating and demoralizing. Moreover, you will catch up: again, be patient with yourself. And be patient with your research. Your first endeavor almost certainly will be your best only if it is your last. Research – and hence doctoral work – is a process, rather than an end goal. Patiently enjoy the process; smile at your successes, and don't worry about your (inevitable) failures. (Incidentally, these seem like fairly good guides for living one's non-research life as well. If there is such a thing ...)

Charles Becker,
Duke University, Economics

Do not lose sight of the primary purpose of your research project, which is your education. While it is of course quite desirable to produce some seminal research during your PhD, chasing this as the primary goal can come at the expense of your development as a researcher. For example, a highly prescriptive project definition with close guidance from your supervisor may be optimal in terms of maximizing the likelihood of producing seminal research, but more freedom and independence will be more beneficial to your development as an independent researcher, allowing you to learn from your wrong turns, and may even lead to a wider range of possible research contributions, being less restricted by your advisor's imagination. This is not to say that more independence is always better: there is a careful balance to be struck between freedom and guidance, but ideally your advisor will help you decide from various directions you have chosen based on an initial project idea they will likely have suggested, as opposed to choosing your directions for you, especially as your project progresses. Similarly, your advisor should be helping you to figure out how to solve your problems, as opposed to solving them for you. Finally, it is important to find a PhD supervisor who puts your development as a researcher ahead of the magnitude of your research contribution. This may be quite difficult to ascertain, but if you have the opportunity to speak to current students in a prospective supervisor's research group, you may be able to get a sense of the nature of the supervision provided.

David Zingg,
University of Toronto,
Computational Aerodynamics

Two often interrelated tendencies stand out for me as behavioral patterns to avoid. The first is a hypercritical sensibility, often fostered by the coursework phase of PhD training. Especially in the humanities and interpretive social sciences, seminars can become an exercise in intellectual Jenga, as students look to pull out what they see as the weak arguments of whatever scholarship they encounter. That approach can accentuate a tendency toward perfectionism and self-doubt once doctoral students embark on their own research. I have never seen a perfect dissertation. But I have seen many brilliant graduate students founder because they could not stop picking holes in their own ideas and arguments, and so struggled to conceptualize a clear narrative arc and then write.

Edward Balleisen,
Duke University, History and Public Policy

Don't be afraid of failure. We all start down the wrong inquiry paths, mess up relationships, and have to recycle whole swaths of our work along the way. Going wrong, even very wrong, is not a reason to stall out. Take stock, reflect on what happened, learn a lesson or two, and get back to writing.

Kim Brooks,
Dalhousie University, Law

One of the best students I worked with was defined by something he didn't do … he didn't take reviews of our research personally, and he didn't let negative reviews bum him out or slow him down. It's very natural to think that paper you submitted is excellent as it is and, when others critique it, it's also natural to get angry or hurt, and that can make you want to avoid thinking about the comments more deeply or revising the paper at all. I've had papers sit for months simply because I was so annoyed by the reviews. This great student of mine, he approached reviews in a very dispassionate, clinical, sort of way. First, he firmly expected all reviewers to raise points we'd need to address, and he expected at least one really nasty review. When they came, he clinically pulled out each of the points and listed them as headings. Then one by one he considered them, considered whether they could be addressed in a revision and, if so, how. Then he made the revision, and noted it in a letter to the editor. Then on to the next one. We might receive the reviews on Thursday, and by Monday he would have revisions done, and a cover letter created. Note, he would do that EVEN IF THE PAPER WAS REJECTED! Why? Because in that case we'd be sending the revised version somewhere else, along with the cover letter noting the revisions. Then even if the paper went back to the original reviewers, they would see that their points were considered and reacted to.

It was eye-opening to me how well this strategy of not getting emotional worked. If we were invited to resubmit, and the paper came back days later with a thoughtful letter to the editor ... the editor still remembered everything and could quickly see that the points were well addressed ... and often it turned into a quick accept. If we had to submit somewhere new, the editor would almost treat it like a revision (heck, it was a reviewer-informed revised version) and sometimes would just send it to one new reviewer.

So don't get mad, get it back ... but do it thoughtfully and things will continue to move along well.

Steve Joordens,
University of Toronto, Psychology

In order to thrive I think it is important that a doctoral student be prepared for rejection and be realistic about their ability to take criticism about their work, especially when it comes to receiving feedback en route to publication. The old adage of "publish or perish" still seems to rule supreme among doctoral candidates and early career researchers. And to a large degree this is one of the primary ways to distinguish among candidates for academic positions. But in order to publish you need to put your work out there. And in putting your work out there through submission to peer reviewed journals you are likely to get rejected more often than not. I recall that early in my program my supervisor encouraged me to publish an article drawn from my Masters work. I dutifully worked it up and sent it off and, months later, I received my first rejection letter. No feedback, and certainly no "revise and resubmit." Just a flat out "no." I was devastated. I slowly walked over to see my supervisor to deliver the news that I had failed him and was unworthy and would be withdrawing from the program right away. When I showed him the rejection letter his immediate response was, "Where will you be sending the manuscript tomorrow?" Huh? He wanted me to send it to another journal the very next day (unchanged, since the first journal gave no feedback). I ended up doing so and this time it was accepted, with some revisions. When I talked to him about it he explained that he assumed it was not a good fit between the article content and the journal, hence "send it somewhere else." It taught me a great lesson about the realities of publishing – the need to get ready for rejection and to press through it. Since then, I've had manuscripts rejected multiple times until I figured out the best revisions and the best fit. Other times I've had manuscripts accepted on the first try with minimal changes. But without being prepared for – braced for – rejection and criticism, and without understanding that I cannot take it personally (it's not about "me"), I would have been crippled early on from making myself vulnerable in this way.

Richard Ascough,
Queen's University, Religion

Avoid beating yourself up. When things go wrong, you're not a failure or a fake. Research is full of errors and false starts. Blaming yourself only ensures there will be more errors and more false starts and more blame – cycles of self-doubt leading only to rigor mortis. Learn, recalibrate, move on.

Randy Allen Harris,
University of Waterloo,
Linguistics, Rhetoric,
and Communication Design

Every PhD student should strive, with resolve and humility, to grow into their best intellectual and professional self in accordance with their unique combination of interests and talents. But what is absolutely foundational to that general aim – and, therefore, required in every case – is the cultivation of one, an appreciation of and tenacious aspiration for excellence; two, an understanding – indeed, internalization – of self as a work in progress; three, a steadfast commitment to intellectual and professional integrity; and four, a delight in professional community and collaborative exchange.

To cultivate an appreciation of, and tenacious aspiration for, excellence. Excellence is not, in my mind, an abstract principle; it is a situated performance. And being excellent is not something one ever is (as in "Mary is excellent" – case closed, work done); instead, excellence is a practice in time, something one does – again and again and never the same. What, I encourage my students to ask themselves, does it mean for me to be an excellent student, today? Given who I am now, what is required of me in this moment to be excellent? PhD students need, in other words, to appreciate excellence (joy may be found there) in any given case and to practice excellence in their daily lives. A situated concept of excellence makes life-long learners of us all.

To cultivate an understanding – indeed, internalization – of self as a work in progress. Grasping oneself as always-becoming or on-the-way rather than as being or will-have-been is doubly productive. In shifting their focus from product to process, students are gifted the freedom of productive play, exploration, revision, and reinvention. But doing so also and at the same time grants them license to be done: the liberating promise of the next word rather than the heavy burden of the last word. Albeit necessarily tethered to an abiding appreciation for excellence (otherwise this can function as excuse structure), self as a work in progress opens the way to being able to say without shame "I don't know" or "I just don't get it yet" or "I've changed my mind" – indispensable on every side.

To cultivate a steadfast commitment to intellectual and professional integrity. With respect to scholarship, this means habituating oneself into producing original work that is as responsible as it is innovative. With respect to teaching, this means persistent effort in delivering first-rate courses that are meaningful for and respectful of their students' lives (it is often necessary to remind young, enthusiastic scholar-teachers that there is more than one valuable life worth living). With respect to their professional lives more generally, this means paying vigilant respect to the hard lesson that the responsibility for our own speech (in the classroom, in meetings with colleagues, in the conference setting, and more) and for our own writing (from emails to applications to recommendations, and more) is irreducible.

To cultivate a delight in professional community and collaborative exchange, the prerequisites of which are a generosity of intellectual spirit and genuine sense of inquiry. There is no small degree to which the scholar's life necessarily is a solitary affair. However, training in the advanced skills necessary to authoring work of one's own is too often purchased, I think, at the expense of regular exchange with a community of one's peers. Reading, thinking, and sharing work in progress with others should not, in my view, stop when formal coursework ends. To the contrary, it is at this stage in the process that all of these activities can have their most profound effects: in writing groups, discovering how to usefully review a piece of someone else's work (preparation for a not so distant future when serving as an ad hoc referee for a journal or panel respondent at a convention is the next step) and learning how to fine-tune one's capacity to effectively answer questions about one's own (preparation for the comprehensive oral exam, the dissertation defense, the conference presentation); in reading groups, finding deep satisfaction in practicing the art of asking a good question (one that demonstrates a generosity of intellectual spirit rather than showmanship) to experiencing the enjoyment of collaborative exchange on the way toward crafting a thoughtful and nuanced answer.

Barbara A. Biesecker,
University of Georgia, Communication Studies

"There is no one-size-fits-all." Each student needs to hear a different piece of advice … I know this, because it's obvious after you've taught for a while, and also because I asked all of my current and former PhD students what I had said to them that best fit this heading – and as I suspected, no two of those who responded returned the same answer! Here are the various pieces of advice that students say were the most important to them:

- Learning is a process; feedback is a gift.
- I remember you sitting me down at the start of my PhD and asking what my goal was (academia) and saying to let you know if things changed and I wanted to pursue a different path (e.g., industry). It was useful to know I had a goal to work toward that I could measure my progress on and decide if I needed to pivot in terms of topic/experience at some point to open up my options. It let me know that the non-academic path isn't a consolation prize; it's something you need to work toward actively if you want it.
- You said to us, "even I still learn, and won't stop learning …"
- Celebrate even the little wins; not so much advice but part of a culture you encourage – normalizing failures, ups and downs as part of the process to help prevent these from being internalized as part of a negative self-concept; emphasizing balance; writing early in the day; set regular meetings; seek feedback early in the study design process and preregister with consideration of analysis – helps identify possible problems early + good for open science; join and get involved in a lab.
- Every PhD student has the same struggles: you are not alone.
- Keep in touch with their primary advisor on a weekly basis – the weekly meetings we had really kept me on

track, otherwise during the difficult periods I would have fallen off the grid and felt worse and worse. Even though some of the meetings were hard when I hadn't progressed much, without them, I would have maybe never finished on time!

- Being explicit in describing expectations, providing feedback, and in writing/speaking style. Another element of your approach was an emphasis on incremental progress … – i.e., the importance of delivering outputs rather than endlessly polishing or reading more papers, etc., because this helped to manage the amount of time you spent on things and allowed for increased productivity. I would add, "you are not your thesis." In some ways this is about self-care and avoiding feelings of guilt and obligation to constantly think about and work on the thesis all the time, or to feel deeply hurt when people criticize or give harsh negative feedback on your work. But it is also about how the PhD time is a chance to dabble in areas and develop skills and networks that reach beyond the specific discipline or topic of your PhD thesis, which can lead to new ideas and connections that shape your research program.
- You always had a really helpful "up and at 'em" attitude when it came to rejections. I think I felt quite inoculated from the pain of them in part because of your normalization of rejection and constructive approach to incorporating the feedback and trying again. That, plus your passion for knowledge and curiosity about the things you (and other people) studied was a very good

> template for me of what a scientist should be. I think you taught me this mindset: rejections aren't about you; they're about figuring out how best to study something. In terms of things to avoid, I'd say an overly defeatist or victim mentality about rejection. Resilience!

Winnifred R. Louis,
University of Queensland, Psychology

Avoid comparing yourself with others. There is real danger here, and ironically it is worse when you have chosen your lab well, and there are stellar people around you. I once fell into a trap where every time someone around me had a success I would only feel more pressure and more stress. My own successes felt small and began to bring less and less pleasure; I perpetually felt like I was falling behind in the race to the top. The feeling didn't lessen when I got tenure. It took me years to learn to define what success looks like for me, and quit judging myself purely by watching the performance of others. Only then did I begin to really enjoy my successes.

Richard Fuller,
University of Queensland, Biology

There are several thought patterns and behaviors that PhD students should avoid. I will share only three here. To begin with, 1) students should avoid the passivity trap – believing that others are responsible for their challenges, and they can do nothing to improve their own situations. Take charge of your doctoral studies as an entrepreneur would take responsibility for creating a new business. You are creating a new career. Work to learn from, improve, and recover from disappointing situations. Persevere. 2) Avoid the other extreme – the "it's all up to me" trap. Students should not be embarrassed to reach out for help (e.g., when they are mentally unwell or in financial difficulties) or for social interaction (e.g., when they feel isolated). Faculty, students, and staff may not notice that help is needed, and some situations may require more resources than the student has. "Help!" is a useful four-letter word. Finally, 3) students should avoid overestimating what can be accomplished and going in multiple directions (e.g., taking on too much additional work for pay, or working on too many different research projects and papers). Avoid distractions and disorganization. Keep the main thing (your courses and research) the main thing. Stay focused on the end goal – your research, publications, and (where appropriate) teaching experience.

Yolande E. Chan,
McGill University, Digital Technology

Avoid listening to advice from those who are not in your program, or working with your supervisor. Avoid comparing yourself and your timeline to others who are doing a different study. Avoid spiraling into the "impostor syndrome" rabbit hole and instead understand that virtually everyone experiences this at some point or another. Avoid thinking you can do no work on your dissertation for months and then expect yourself to be able to do it in a week because the end of term is approaching. Avoid expecting perfection of yourself – the PhD is your opportunity to learn. Avoid thinking the draft is the final version. Avoid a "fixed mindset" as you progress – as things are bound to change in your thinking, your life, or your circumstances.

Kathryn Hibbert,
Western University, Education

Perfection does not exist! Fortunately, otherwise, all research would be final and definitive. Wanting to do too well can be paralyzing or demotivating because we do not accept the risks inherent to adventure. Not seeking perfection at all costs does not however exclude the need for rigor and a commitment to quality, both of which are required for a doctorate; it is more a question of accepting that meticulousness has its limits.

Your work will inspire others to pursue or to study certain aspects further, to explore other angles; indeed, it might inspire you too, seeing as a thesis, though very important, does not constitute your life's work. A thesis represents a significant milestone, but it is not a final professional project. Also, the exchange between your supervisor and yourself, as well as with your colleagues, is crucial to a healthy confrontation of ideas; above all the goal remains enrichment, growth, and progress. Don't be discouraged and don't disparage yourself. Fame is not a primary goal; the important thing is that you propose a significant contribution. Nurture your equilibrium, your serenity, your determination to continue your journey with an accomplished project that shows your abilities and your perseverance.

Jocelyne Mathieu,
Université Laval, History

Don't take rejection (of manuscripts, research ideas, grant and scholarship applications) personally as a statement of your value to your discipline or your future in becoming a colleague. Initial reaction to criticism, even that which is meant to be helpful, is often defensive or defeatist. Constructive feedback is valuable in achieving your career path and in developing a realistic plan. Hone and fine tune your goals, craft clearer and more focused perspectives. Keep in mind that even negative or seemingly less than enthusiastic feedback during your PhD program can be a good learning opportunity to appreciate differing insights and research concerns from colleagues and colleagues-in-training. Simply put for PhD students – use criticism and feedback to your advantage. Reframe negatives into positive research and teaching lessons, giving you insights into your own biases, assumptions, and values which you have as a colleague-in-training. Think of constructive feedback as a positive "call to action" in your PhD career development.

Laurie Hoffman-Goetz,
University of Waterloo, Anthropology

We generally begin a PhD project full of energy, highly motivated, and with a certain amount of pride. Being accepted into a doctoral program is a significant achievement in itself. Reaching this milestone shows that you are tenacious, able to carry out long-term projects, and willing to put considerable effort into them.

Being admitted into a PhD program is a genuine milestone; finishing your PhD, however, is a much greater challenge. The data show it: drop-out rates for PhD students are quite high, and the reasons for this many and varied. This being the case, why not engage in a bit of prevention? The most valuable experience that I can pass on to doctoral students is that, one day, whatever the PhD project, you will run into a wall, a wall that you cannot sidestep, a wall that you must climb over in order to continue. This wall will cause you a great deal of doubt about the continuation of your project: Have I reached my limits? Do I have what it takes?

The nature of the wall is often not foreseeable. And because we did not see it coming, it can be all the more destabilizing. It may come to you as a difficulty in grasping a complex theory, a participant recruitment that takes forever, a study grant that you are not awarded, a first version of a thesis whose progress is considered to be insufficient, an article that is refused, or the overwhelming feelings involved in reconciling one's roles as a doctoral student, partner, and parent. The list is long …

What is different about those who finish their PhD? The day they saw the obstacle before them, they said, "That's the wall." (This usually occurs AFTER supervisors help students to see the situation from another angle.) The wall does not represent the end of the journey. Rather, it is a time to invest new energy, organize the work differently, and look for support. Above all, it is part and parcel of a NORMAL PhD trajectory.

So, is it worth all the effort? Definitely, because a PhD is also the art of learning how to overcome obstacles. Doing a PhD prepares you to become a researcher. There are moments of great satisfaction in this career: contributing to our understanding of complex phenomena, helping to find answers that shed light on the potential options, getting a grant, being published in a journal that we particularly respect. But it also comprises all sorts of hurdles, refusals, and constraints in time and money. Nelson Mandela once said, "May your choices reflect your hopes, not your fears." When doing a PhD, our hope is to successfully defend our thesis. So, let's go. We start climbing and we overcome the vertigo!

Marie-Christine Saint-Jacques,
Université Laval, Law

Most PhD candidates embark on their studies with grand aspirations. Everything will be done just right. You aim to start academic life the way you mean to go on throughout your career, in short, perfectly. You will avoid mistakes, detours, delays, and other instances of perceived failure at all costs. This kind of thinking is understandable, most of us have been there. And the sentiment driving this thought pattern comes from a good place. It is born out of motivation, from enthusiasm for the project, for the opportunity to excel, or to make the world a slightly better place. And what better time to start your immaculate track record as an academic than at that monumental milestone, the start of becoming a "proper" academic, right? Maybe not. It is a truism that perfection is the enemy of good, the enemy of progress, the enemy of Done, or even the enemy of excellence. But maybe there is something to the platitude after all. Among much else, the PhD is a time for curiosity, a time for exploration, a time to extend oneself and one's thinking, a time to trial new ways of intellectual engagement. Will stretching oneself to new limits entail experiences of failure? Probably, yes. But the opportunity cost of perfectionism may be immense. By imposing a paradigm of perfectionism on what is a significant opportunity for personal and professional growth, you are limiting your chances to benefit from much of what PhD study is all about.

Julia N. Albrecht,
University of Otago, Business

REFLECTION AND APPLICATION ACTIVITIES

The advice in this chapter addresses challenge and failure head-on with concrete advice on how to overcome and persevere. First and foremost are strategies to adjust your mindset, to accept obstacles, avoid comparisons, learn and grow, and embrace feedback. "Measure" Your Growth is a personalized reflection on your current growth mindset. Take your time with it and be honest as you explore areas where you can improve. Approach the activity with a growth mindset! Mindset Intervention presents a research-based opportunity to improve your mindset, while supporting a continuous improvement culture.

Activity 1: "Measure" Your Growth

There are quizzes available online to help ascertain how strong your growth mindset is. However, this activity is personalized: designed to help you cultivate *your* growth mindset, based on your current state.

1. Consider each component of the growth mindset and find evidence in your professional life of both fixed and growth mindsets. Thinking of each row as a continuum from completely fixed mindset to completely growth-oriented mindset, rank yourself on a scale of 0–10, with 10 being 100 per cent growth-oriented for that element.

Fixed Mindset	Evidence	Growth Mindset	Evidence	Rating (0–10)
Gives up easily		Persists in setbacks		
Avoids challenges		Embraces challenges		
Sees effort as fruitless		Sees effort as the way to mastery		
Avoids negative feedback		Embraces criticism as a means to learn		
Others' success is a threat		Others' success is a source of learning		

2. Review the evidence and your ratings and choose one or two areas that you'd like to improve. Everyone is growing, so you're unlikely to have a 10 for every element. For each improvement area, jot down some of your typical self-talk in a relevant situation. Finally, replace the current self-talk with equivalent but improved thoughts. We've provided an example to get you started.

Area for Growth	Relevant Situation	Current Self-Talk	Replacement Self-Talk
Persisting in the face of setbacks	I've worked on multiple drafts of a paper and I don't want to change it again based on my supervisor's comments.	This is good enough. Why am I being made to repeat this work? I'll never get this right.	This is a steppingstone on the way to mastery. People commenting on my work think I can perform better. They want to help me get there. As I continue to learn, I will reach further heights! I have not yet mastered this.

Activity 2: Mindset Intervention

One of the interventions found to influence students' growth mindset was teaching other students about it. Take up the challenge and educate others about the growth mindset, be it family, friends, colleagues, or – as in the research study – someone who is not as far along in their academic journey. You might have a conversation, write a blog, letter, or email. You might do an assignment on the growth mindset, conduct a workshop or tutorial, or take some time in your regular teaching activities or mentorship role to educate students. Use the following chart to plan.

Who's my audience?

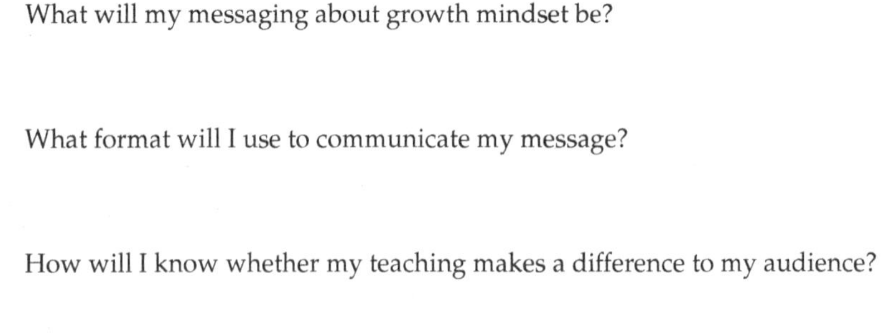

What will my messaging about growth mindset be?

What format will I use to communicate my message?

How will I know whether my teaching makes a difference to my audience?

Once you've communicated the impact of a growth mindset, reflect on how the experience influences your own thinking by asking *How might I react in future to setbacks?*

Activity 3: The Three Rs of Reflection

Recall: I Must Remember

What are my top takeaways from this chapter?

Revise: What Do I Want to Do Differently?

Based on the advice from this chapter, what is most important for me to personally change or improve? Write down a commitment for one small action you will do differently right away.

Reimagine: What Do I Hope Will Happen?

Reimagining a future reality for ourselves and setting clear intentions is powerful in changing our current practices and achieving our goals. Based on the advice from this chapter, describe a vision of yourself in the future. A prompt for this exercise: *In one year, I hope …*

CHAPTER EIGHT

Believe in Yourself

"Believe in yourself. No one else will."

Whoa – that's a cynical idea! It's also untrue. In fact, our social minds might actually work in a way that's opposite to that statement. It's more likely that "if you believe in yourself, others will believe in you." Imagine you have just survived a small plane crash and are stranded on a remote beach with a small group of strangers. The pilot is unconscious.

"We need to set a flare," a man in a fine suit says, looking around.

"I'm not sure I'd be able to do that," says the woman with long dark hair who sat beside you and told you all about her work as a nurse.

"I know how to set flares," says the woman who was sitting behind you. Her neon green sneakers catch your eye. She rolls up her sleeves.

Are you going to put your trust in the person who says they are confident about how to set a flare, or the person who is not so sure? Likely the confident person; it's a logical choice.

It is natural for people to take cues about who you are based on how you behave and speak. Signaling to others that you are competent results in them assuming you *are* competent. The simplest way to signal that you are competent is to believe you are competent. This belief, or judgment of your own capability of accomplishing a particular task, is known as *self-efficacy*.

The term self-efficacy was coined by social psychologist Albert Bandura,[1] and defined as "judgments of how well one can execute courses of action required to deal with prospective situations" (Bandura, 1982, p. 122).[2] Self-efficacy, one's belief in one's competence, has a strong influence on performance. Put another way: if you believe you can do something, you are more likely to be motivated to put in the effort and achieve it to a high standard. A myriad of studies demonstrates the relationship between self-efficacy and performance in a wide variety of settings including organizational work settings[3] such as academia,[4] education,[5] and more.[6]

While high performance is imperative in academic environments, there are yet more reasons to pay attention to believing in yourself. Self-esteem has been linked to lower impacts of stress,[7] greater resilience,[8] and making healthy choices.[9] This makes sense: if you believe you can maintain a healthy exercise regime, eat well, and avoid unhealthy habits, then you are much more likely to put effort into these healthy routines. Failure is uncomfortable – we avoid it. And, if we fail once, we are more likely to avoid trying again. For example, research shows that a key factor in the success of someone quitting smoking is their belief that they *can* quit smoking.[10]

There's another obvious consequence of believing in yourself: it's easier to be persistent in achieving something others do not think possible. At one point in time, 1954 to be exact, running a mile in less than four minutes was thought impossible. If Roger Bannister agreed with these naysayers, it would never have happened. What if Elvis Presley didn't believe in himself, but instead listened to the band leader who rejected him as a vocalist and told him to stick to truck driving? People also said the lightbulb was impossible, the X-ray, getting to the moon, the airplane, the smartphone, and so on. "You have to believe in yourself when no one else does – that makes you a winner right there," said Venus Williams. She echoed the words of Sugar Ray Robinson, "to be a champ you have to believe in yourself when no one else will." Believing in yourself is a prerequisite for any extraordinary achievement.

By now you might be thinking: believing in yourself sounds great, but there's a big difference between understanding the value of self-efficacy and *actually* having it, particularly in a PhD where imposter syndrome is rampant and praise hard to come by. Where are you supposed to *get* it – especially during the difficult times? We have good news: while people's concept of you can have a negative effect on your self-efficacy, so too can people's positive concept of you enhance your self-efficacy.[11] In other words, when your belief in yourself wanes, the belief of others in you can be a good substitute. In fact, others' belief in you can have positive, lasting impacts. For example, in research about what encourages and discourages creativity, the beliefs of others had a significant impact on participants' belief in their ability to be creative, with long-lasting consequences.[12]

Most of us have people in our lives who believe in us. And if you don't – it's time to go find some. When you feel the claws of self-doubt clutching at you, go to those you trust and ask them to remind you of the ways they believe in your competence.

There are many other means to enhance self-belief, and the advice from supervisors in this chapter is tailored to the challenges faced by those pursuing a doctorate. We also recommend a little book called *100 Ways to Boost Your Self-Confidence: Believe in Yourself and Others Will Too* by psychologist and author Barton Goldsmith.[13] Some of the advice Goldsmith gives could be categorized as "fake it till you make it," or taking on the behaviors and habits of people who already have a lot of self-confidence. There are plenty of videos and articles online that provide tips and strategies to "appear" confident. Can these make a difference? We think so: because if you act confident about your performance, people will believe you can perform, and that will positively reinforce your confidence – for real. Formally known as a self-fulfilling prophecy,[14] someone's beliefs about another can cause the other to behave in ways in keeping with the belief, thus making it come true after all. A classic example is the teacher who decides a pupil is less competent than they are, and the student responds by behaving in a way that meets the teacher's false expectations.

There's a caveat to this entire discussion about believing in yourself, and that's falling into the trap of being overly confident. It's all too easy to do, as a well-known study in 2022 demonstrated when 25 per cent of participants who watched a three-minute YouTube video of a pilot landing a plane believed they could also land a plane to the same standard as a professional.[15] A lot of people are, apparently, overconfident in their abilities. There's a pattern by which those who exhibit the most overconfidence are also the least competent. It's called the Dunning-Kruger effect;[16] basically, these people are so bad at something that they have no idea how bad they are. They are unconsciously incompetent.

Should you worry about being overconfident? Not really. Overconfidence is generally beneficial,[17] unless you're in a dangerous situation where lives are at stake, such as landing a plane, caring for a patient in a hospital, or handling a lethal pathogen. Being aware of the potential for overconfidence can't hurt though, and most PhD students reading this book are likely to be suffering from a lack of confidence, not the other way around. Hence the advice about believing in yourself given in this chapter by supervisors from around the world.

ADVICE ON BELIEVING IN YOURSELF

The biggest trap is when you doubt yourself. You were chosen. You were picked from among a pool of applicants who were smart and driven. You are the one sitting in that office interacting with undergrads and trying to keep your head above water. Don't fall for the imposter syndrome. It will make you question yourself and everything that you do. You can't see it now, but you will succeed. You will finish. Yes, it will be painful, and it may take a long time. But you will finish.

Remember that perfection isn't the goal. You need to pass. That's all. Do your work as well as you can and if you have concerns, find a mentor who will listen to you, pat you on the back when you need support, hold your hand when you cry, and look sternly at you because you start talking about quitting. That being said, if you don't see that the work for the PhD is what you thought it would be, be honest with yourself. If you don't want it, then stop. Leave. Quit. It's worse to do something you hate than to find something that brings you joy.

Bonnie L. Youngs,
Carnegie Mellon University,
French & Francophone Studies for Modern Languages

Comparisons are odious. Do not compare yourself to others if it instills self-doubt or loathing or paralysis. The endpoint of academia and doctoral studies is arguably to make a contribution to knowledge, your contribution to knowledge, with a view to positively enhancing and understanding the world and to also developing yourself. Life is abstract and is wholly subjective. There will be dissenters and critics. As academics and researchers, we are teaching ourselves to understand the world in a rigorous, thorough, reasoned, and methodical way. We are being discerning and probing, thorough and meticulous, so that we might, among other things, be respected by dissenters and critics, as well as our supporters. We are measuring ourselves against the standards that others have set for us, whether these standards emerged thousands of years ago, say through scripture, whether these standards have been enculturated through the development of legislation, or whether these standards have arisen through the academic peer review process! These forms of standard-setting are useful in academia as they help us to be excellent and to make positive contributions to the world. Yet, what is less useful is negative comparison, pointless comparison, odious comparison. This is destructive, negative, and oftentimes internally driven and subjective. Do not listen to other students when you are facing self-doubt, when they are saying how many amazing pages of brilliant research they have produced, or how much better their work is than yours. Do not compare yourselves to others. There are many, very different ways that people learn and think and see things. So instead of comparing yourself to other people, the focus for you should be on working toward understanding different peoples' perspectives. Students work and learn at different paces and in different ways so this can be like comparing apples and oranges! The only person to compare yourself to is you. Where have you come from, what have you achieved, how have you overcome challenges, what are your triumphs and achievements, how do you behave toward others? Be influenced by positive people, role models, and supporters. Aim to be like someone for positive reasons, but do not compare yourself for negative reasons.

Karen Makuch,
Imperial College London, Environmental Politics

For me, after struggling to settle on "the single, most important piece of advice" (I'd concede that there are numerous helpful pieces of advice such as always back up your work, exercise regularly, eat well, have a social life, write down your flashes of inspiration ...), I would suggest that having unwavering self-belief is central to you fulfilling your potential as a PhD student. Not a conceited, arrogant form of self-belief, where you are closed off to advice and support, or where you are dismissive of others' views and experiences, but one where you can draw from deep inside of yourself when you feel low, or feel criticized, or question yourself or others question you or your work. An unwavering form of self-belief, that you can draw from when you feel that you might not complete the research, or that you have run out of ideas, or failed to write more than one line in eight hours, will propel you. An unwavering sense of self-belief, where you know deep in your mind or in the bottom of your heart that you can do this, will allow you to be at your creative best and "go for it" in terms of being innovative and inspired, being bold enough to make your mark and confident enough in your work. This self-belief is partly something that has to come from within you, but if your PhD supervisor is good at their job, they will bring this out of you and help you grow and flower. Could this unwavering form of self-belief be described as tenacity? Is it drive? Is it focus? Is it determination? Perhaps self-belief is the sense that precedes these concepts, for you cannot develop drive or focus or tenacity or determination without an inherent and unwavering "something" from inside of you. This "something" is the seed that will have been planted deep inside you during your life – from teachers who supported you, from parents who nurtured you, from friends who understood you. It's there … just let it flourish! "When you do things from your soul, you feel a river moving in you, a joy." – Rumi

Karen Makuch,
Imperial College London, Environmental Politics

Avoid invidious comparisons of self with others. In the goldfish bowl that a graduate department can be, messages implicit and explicit that consecrate the golden few as Ideal PhD Candidates can be misleading and even, I would say, harmful. The colleague who always seems able to stun the graduate seminar with a comment that lands with brilliant éclat is not necessarily the best thinker in the room (as a long-time graduate seminar instructor, I can assure you of this). The system is, alas, constructed so as to promote such invidious comparisons: Who has rich external funding and who does not? Who always seems to be on the conference circuit? etc. Mindfully identify these messages, as a first step in objectifying them, and then make every effort you can to block them. In her wonderful book *Keep It Moving: Lessons for the Rest of Your Life*, the American choreographer Twyla Tharp distinguishes between creating "cathedrals," the monumental successes, and creating "bridges," the working products that allow us to hone our craft. We often, as working academics, feel the pressure to create the "cathedral," the perfect performance, whether that's a brilliant PhD thesis, a successful tutorial class, a lauded conference paper or article, or that seminar comment that lands with brilliant éclat. Furthermore, we are often convinced that the people sitting beside us are creating cathedrals while we toil away at our rickety bridges. But Tharp, who, at seventy-eight, says she's created a handful of "cathedrals" in her long and distinguished career, looks with affection and approval on her other works, imperfect bridges that were helping her to hone her choreographic skills and take her somewhere new. Her reflection, "When I can't build a cathedral, I build a bridge to get there," is one I would both agree with and revise. Those whom we assume are building cathedrals may simply be adept at the art of assembling a glittery facade. For that matter, I'd take a bridge over a cathedral anytime: a work that calls out to a community to collaborate in a work of thinking rather than to a passive audience to gasp in wonder at our skill. Walter Benjamin wrote that "An author who teaches writers nothing teaches no one. What matters [is to] be able … to induce other producers to produce," and I think the same holds true for academic labor. So, avoid the invidious comparisons with the putative cathedral-builders out there and, together with your cohort of people who nourish you, build bridges.

Lorraine York,
McMaster University, Canadian Literature

When asked what advice and support they valued in supervision, several students valued my support in their struggle for self-confidence. The advice that mattered thus included:

- Try to avoid putting yourself down/self-deprecation
- Avoid thinking "you are not enough"

- Comparison with others. We all do it and are all told not to do it, but it is very destructive; imposter syndrome thought patterns are also super important to avoid; Self-sabotaging!

Winnifred R. Louis,
University of Queensland, Psychology

If there was just the one piece of advice that to some degree embraces all the others, it would be that you must take ownership of your project. At the end of the PhD, you should be a world expert in the subarea and be the person driving the field by asking new questions and opening new avenues. It is commonly all too easy to slip into a mode where you can do the techniques and (hopefully) produce good data, but at the same time not "own" the project. You can become both myopically focused and turn into a data generating machine. The difference would be that the owner of a project is thinking not just about the technical hurdles, but the bigger picture. They are reading around and questioning why it matters. Crucially, they are not simply doing whatever the PI tells them to do, but they are seeing the next question (and not uncommonly why the PI is an idiot). Importantly, you need to think about your data and what it means. In this context my other advice would be to be honest to the data. Often people have an idea what the outcome of an investigation should be. Often the data do not agree. When there is a conflict between expectation and data, go with the data. Don't try and force it to align with some prior model or indeed "textbook" wisdom. It isn't simply the case that science is most exciting when the data don't seem to be as expected – this is when conventional "wisdom" gets overturned. But forcing data into preexisting models is just bad science – let the data tell you the "story." A further critical component of this "honesty" is that you also need to be sure your data is good data. It is very seductive to turn bad data into a novel story. I've seen too many high-profile papers based on poor data where the authors really should have properly scrutinized the results. You will know in your heart of hearts if you are accepting second rate data to spin a sexy narrative. Good science also means being your sternest and most honest critic.

Laurence Hurst,
University of Bath, Evolutionary Genetics

Follow your passion. Identify a research question that ignites your curiosity, one that moves both heart and mind. Sometimes this topic may be clearly connected to a world problem and a desire for social change. Sometimes the question demands aesthetic investigation, and the outcome may be an artistic project with less obvious application. Sometimes, your question may be so specifically focused on theory, it is not immediately clear how it can contribute to anything beyond that theory. Regardless, insist that the question you define as significant to you remains your question even as it is finely honed or changes radically over the course of your degree program. You are the one doing this work: you are the one ultimately responsible for the outcome.

Find a supervisor and committee members who bring varied scholarly strength to support the breadth and depth of your research interests and who will insist on the rigor of that work. Of course, as you read your way through existing scholarship and study in classes with your professors, your passions and your research question may shift and change. Embrace that change even as it deepens the inquiry and takes you in unanticipated directions. It can be especially rewarding to find professors who revel in your potential to challenge them, taking their ideas (and yours) to another level – beyond what they might have done without you. Working on a PhD especially when you get to the final stages can be some of the loneliest work you will ever do. Remind yourself frequently of your reasons for the line of inquiry you are pursuing. Write to communicate those thoughts that matter to you. Thriving through the process comes with maintaining the passion and staying true to yourself.

Celia Haig-Brown,
York University, Education

Avoid letting fear stop you from writing your good ideas down. Step through the looking glass. When you are an undergraduate student, you learned to be excellent by reading as much as you could. As you synthesized ideas and saw patterns in other people's work you could craft a story and put it together. That is why you are doing your PhD. You have already shown you can write well about the known work in a field. It can also stop you from taking the next step which is to write about what is not yet well known in your field. At some stage you need to step from the land of the known, and synthesizing what others think, and through the looking glass into the unknown and start proposing new ideas and new knowledge. Fear can whisper – who am I to say what is missing from the field? Anxiety can shout – what if others disagree? Yet your PhD is about creating new knowledge. No one else will have read the combination of things you have read and gathered data in the time and place and way that you have. Your writing is a conversation with others to advance your field. PhD writing is all kinds of big and small pieces and many, many drafts so don't hesitate. Your explanations and ideas that are founded on your deep reading, investigating, and thinking are a gift to others.

Jill Willis,
Queensland University of Technology, Education

Avoid comparing yourself to other students (and eventually faculty) in your program. I say this as someone who married a fellow student in my graduate program, and we are now both tenured faculty in the same department. Different kinds of research programs develop different research profiles. Your peers may be doing different kinds of research and so to compare yourself may one day make you feel good, but another day make you feel terrible. Your success is not infringed upon by others' success. Ultimately, the better people do around you, the better the reputation of your program, and the better it is for everyone.

If you want to check in about milestones or progress, ask your advisor and/or mentor. They will be much better judges of your work than any self-comparisons you could do against peers. There are many different versions of what success looks like in the academy. You and your advisor/

mentors will help you figure out what success will look like for you.

Lee Humphreys,
Cornell University, Communications

Students must avoid putting their advisors on a pedestal. Key to a successful student-advisor relationship is for the student to be able to challenge what the advisor says. The advisor was once a PhD student too, and may not have been a particularly good one. I was a hopeless graduate student! But my advisors helped me no end, and I was certainly never afraid to ask them any questions – however naïve.

Tim Coulson,
University of Oxford, Zoology

The best advice I have received from one of my senior professors when I was a doctoral student is "PhD is an endurance process." Based on my own experience, working with about twenty students through my career, I fully agree with this statement. Thus, PhD students should avoid questioning themselves and considering discontinuing the PhD program every time they run into a seemingly formidable hurdle. To this end, it is important to crystalize the reason for pursuing a PhD degree from the very beginning. This will make it easier to stick to the program and see the light at the end of the tunnel without consistently self-criticizing. If you do not have what it takes to complete your PhD, I can assure you that you will hear about it from your supervisors.

Vedat Verter,
Queen's University, Business

Never believe those who say, "You can't do that here." There are always – almost always – strategies to ensure that you can approach your research questions in ways that others may never have anticipated. Universities strive to be places of innovation and invention and creation even as we consistently build on the thought and work of those who came before us. While challenging convention is not for the faint of heart, if you really are committed to the research question that brought you to the university and a related and necessary methodology, you will find strategies that resonate most strongly with you. Very often, the scholars who have the most to teach us are those who push the limits of knowledge, of convention, and of form.

In identifying a supervisor, do not succumb to those who would force you to follow only their lead. Working with experts in their fields is indubitably inspirational but do not feel you must or even can become like them. Remembering the passion that brought you to the university, take what they have to offer to your thinking and the refinement of your own research and leave the hero worship in its rightful place. Similarly, in staying true to yourself, never try to assume a writerly stance that you think is appropriate for a scholar, even one you admire. Rather sift through available words that will allow you to communicate in your own voice with clarity in language that is appropriate to your research question, exploration, and subsequent writing.

Celia Haig-Brown,
York University, Education

Resist the twin temptations of academic life: to become utterly self-referential, and to relinquish to others the determination of the value of your work and of you. These two orientations constitute a Lincoln log of sorts. They are two ends of the same distorted perspective on graduate education and the scholarly life. Both arise from a zero-sum mentality that sees achievement, recognition, and affirmation as scarce, fixed resources. Both presume competition is the fundamental building block of social relationships. Both isolate, constrain, and constrict. Both suck life out of graduate students and professors. Both kill the play and experiences of delight that mark the work of the greatest scholars and teachers. Both impede creative scholarly work. Both diminish individual dignity.

To the extent that you can, resist these temptations, even when they are deeply embedded in the culture of your program. Hold yourself and your work lightly and gently. Respect your work and yourself. Honor your aspirations and live with the reality that they may not be realized. Be faithful to the work. Chop the wood and carry the water, savor the steps on the journey. Don't deceive yourself into thinking that you can plan, control, and predict the narrative of your life and career, whether by winning everything on your own terms or by becoming servilely obedient to your graduate director. There are no guarantees. The narrative arc of your life and scholarly career will unfold like the narrative spine of a novel, and it will surprise you.

Patricia O'Connell Killen,
Pacific Lutheran University, Religion

Avoid comparing yourself with others. Learn to collaborate. Commiserate as necessary. But don't compare because everyone is different.

It's easy enough to say, "Avoid feeling like an imposter!" Amidst the pressures and stress of facing new and intense challenges, our emotions and self-doubts can overwhelm us. There will always be someone further along. Don't get caught up in thinking that the PhD is a competition or a race with only one winner.

Think of it as a banquet: everyone brings something different to the table. There is enough room at the table for everyone and you belong. Your admission into the PhD program was your invitation to the table. Now, lean into conversations, learn to listen, share your voice, and build meaningful and authentic relationships with your peers, with faculty, and scholars in your field and beyond.

The PhD can naturally feel solitary and isolating. It is true that your writing won't get done unless you sit yourself down and do it. Keep showing up even when it is hard. Avoid sitting by yourself and eating alone, particularly when you are overwhelmed. Bring your whole self to the table. Take advantage of the opportunity to engage with other curious, creative, and critical individuals. Explore new ideas and ways of thinking and cultivate relationships that will sustain you throughout your journey as a doctoral student. Some of them will become kindred spirits, dear colleagues, and mentors throughout your career.

Gail Prasad,
York University, Education

Trust yourself. The most important element in the program is you, and no matter how at sea you feel, how overwhelmed by the volume of information, how bamboozled by the access to your material, and how nervous of the prospect of writing, and how deflated you feel at what comes out, remember this: That you chose the topic because it is significant, it has merit, and the research is worth doing. And your supervisors supported and selected you because we were persuaded by the case that you put, and we believe in the intrinsic value and importance of your endeavor. It is hard to sustain the effort, enthusiasm, and joyfulness for study, and easy as the doctoral program proceeds to wonder why you started. In that situation remember to trust yourself and to trust the development of your ideas. Your supervisors also know that exactly how you approach and analyze the topic will change as the program proceeds and your experience increases. And that should be trusted too. The doctoral program has its outputs, but the process is the most important aspect. And the key to that is learning how to trust your judgments and to have confidence in what you've undertaken.

Giles Gasper,
Durham University, High Medieval History

Let us begin with the thesis director: so many want their students to be just like them … mini-mes. This is fine if your thesis director is a saint and you want to be just like him or her and you have no personality of your own. But, if you are to grow within the program, be it a course, a research project, a master's thesis, or a doctorate, then your own development must be paramount and that means you have to establish yourself as a living, thinking, analyzing entity from the start (or as soon as possible after starting).

How you do this is up to you, but I suggest that work on original material is more important than immersion in second-hand theory. Read the academic texts by all means, pay attention to what they say, and by all means see and understand what others have said. But never be a parrot. Put the texts to the acid test of their original meaning, not the interpretations given to them by others. While "texts" refers to the humanities, it can also refer to the social sciences, and where science is concerned, substitute the gathering and examination of raw materials for texts.

"Please, sir, what do you want me to write about" works … but infinitely preferable is the presentation of an original idea and the search for a director who will generously and willingly help you develop that idea. Reducing this to a simplicity: emphasize the importance of primary sources over secondary bibliography on those sources. And remember, if you always accept and believe in authority, you will never find it easy to challenge that authority, even when it is mistaken. If you know your prime material intimately, you can see the errors that the "great authorities" have committed. No, the Earth is not flat. No, the Sun does not go round the Earth. No, the Sun is not pulled by four horses. No, lovely as the idea is, the planets do not dance to music played by a heavenly hand. As Miguel de Cervantes once wrote: *Amicus Platon sed maior amica veritas.* Plato is a friend, but the truth is a greater friend. Listen carefully to what you are being told. Judge carefully and make your own decisions. And remember the words of Oscar Wilde, "Be yourself: everyone else is taken."

Roger Moore,
St. Thomas University,
Spanish Language and Literature

Be sincere, hardworking, and honest toward the work. PhD students need to have out-of-box thinking in a logical manner. They ask questions themselves like *What, Why, How*. They should have a culture of writing down the good things for future needs. After reading many works of their interest, they often get confused and do not get the right direction to move. Consult your peers or supervisor on the topics that will surely release your tension.

Why sincerity and hard work? There is no substitute for sincerity and hard work. Try to love the work with passion rather than pressure. Keep smiling and keep on doing and discussing. Imagination and logical questions with answers will keep you moving in the right direction.

Try to be creative and to avoid losing yourself.

Sri Niwas Singh,
Indian Institute of Technology Kanpur,
Electrical Engineering

The Greek root of the word "idiot" means "self," and nothing turns people off academics like self-regarding arrogance. Many PhD students suffer from a self-effacing lack of confidence, and that brings its own challenges. Others unfortunately develop over-confidence. Never lose sight of the fact that you are one of many contributors to a very wide-ranging conversation that's been going on for some considerable time. This is the case whatever your academic discipline. Your contribution may be valuable, but it will not be unique, nor is it likely to be groundbreaking, regardless of what a gushing audience member might say at an academic conference. It is very easy to experience PhD research as a quest for personal affirmation, and the process of completing a thesis involves so much personal effort, time, and dedication that you'll understandably feel profoundly invested in the project by the time it's over. But while your project might feel like the most important thing in the world, always take some time on a regular basis to remind yourself that it's not. This is an important lesson in humility and perspective. It also underlines how all academic work takes place within a community, and that your own work builds on and depends on that of others. You're contributing to a conversation, one that will continue long after you've finished your PhD. Remembering this is a valuable means of fostering a capacity for communication, respect, and collegiality. In turn, these qualities will make you a better researcher and a more employable graduate.

Mathew Guest,
Durham University, Sociology of Religion

Take ownership of the project and be passionate about the topic to ensure that the research experience is both challenging and enjoyable. While there is a strongly collaborative element in the supervisory relationship, with supervisors offering guidance and making suggestions, the responsibility for defining the project and for making theoretical and methodological choices lies with the doctoral researcher. Even the most brilliant scholars struggle at times, but passion for the topic is essential in having the confidence to take ownership and being able to navigate through moments of toil or difficulty.

Cheryl McEwan,
Durham University, Geography

Forge your own destiny. This is your life, your PhD – you work for yourself, not for your advisor! The reality is that you have the biggest stake in your PhD of anyone on planet Earth. A student has one principal advisor, but your principal advisor likely has a number of PhD students, and definitely has many pressing demands on their time. If you have chosen well, they will be smart but busy. Use their capabilities wisely, tap them for what they are good at – go elsewhere for stuff they are no good at. You know – the internet, the literature, that amazing postdoc down the corridor. Your advisor wants you to succeed, but you are the only one who can make it happen. Take the initiative, suggest ideas, join the dots, make progress between meetings, look for funding or training opportunities, reach out for advice. Your destiny is in your hands.

Richard Fuller,
University of Queensland, Biology

Have confidence in yourself. Work hard and learn to take criticism, but have confidence. If you write a paper or chapter that seems muddled (and we all do that from time to time) don't throw it out. Read it carefully, as if it were written by someone else, to figure out what you were trying to say, and then redraft it so you can say it better. Trust your instincts, even if they are not always clear. And if after several careful readings, you still have not figured out what you were trying to say, put the file in a folder named something like "hopeless first drafts" and start again.

And learn to take criticism. What I mean by this is learn to listen to criticism. Identify what problems in your work the criticism is aimed at. Sometimes a reader (even an advisor) will give advice that is ill-advised. Never ignore advice from someone who has gone to the trouble to critique your work but think of advice as the beginning of a dialogue. If someone who is smart and well-intentioned does not understand your argument, you are not articulating it clearly enough. Form a dissertation reading group with your peers – they will provide you with excellent feedback. You will learn a lot about the genre of dissertation by reading the work of your peers. You learn to write in a genre by reading in a genre, and the dissertation is a peculiar genre.

Learn to take pleasure in your work. There is not pleasure in all of the work. Formatting and footnoting, for example, are pretty much devoid of pleasure. But find the aspects of the work that give you pleasure and spend time on them.

Recognize that a dissertation is not a book. As you are beginning to plan your dissertation, read several dissertations in your field. This will help you understand what a good dissertation is, and what it isn't. It isn't a book.

Learn to really really listen. Being a really fine listener and a really good reader are parallel skills. Think about what this scholar/student is saying and why they are saying it now, in this moment. Who are they responding to? Why are they formulating the statement in the way they are?

Ann Waltner,
University of Minnesota, History

Instead of saying "do this … do that," a student should be encouraged to say "I can do this … I can do that." Sometimes students are afraid to be open with their supervisors and do not open their mouth even when they are right. A supervisor must create an environment for a student to speak their views. Many times, students fear that their idea/work is not correct and they hide it. A supervisor must listen to their view and critically and politely accept if the student is right or be convinced in a logical manner if the student is wrong. This will lead to an environment conducive to good research.

Sri Niwas Singh,
Indian Institute of Technology Kanpur,
Electrical Engineering

Avoid letting your supervisors tell you what to do. This is your PhD not theirs. They are there to advise not to instruct you. You will hear conflicting advice, but the final decisions are yours. A PhD is about you developing the skills to ask and answer questions that matter to you. Don't be a passive recipient of advice. The ideal supervisory session is when you are asking as many questions as your supervisors, so come prepared with your own questions and potential solutions. Draw on their experience to help you make your PhD something you can be proud of while accepting it will never be perfect.

Andrew Hayward,
University College London,
Epidemiology and Public Health

Students should try to avoid conforming to uniform expectations. There are already tens, if not hundreds, of students who want so much to fit with the "academic crowd" in order to be accepted as a "worthy" and "competent" scholar or potential colleague that they all act and speak alike. In fact, it often feels as if they were all the same individual, with little distinction from one another. Thus, students have to find their divergence, their unique trait that will make them stand out and make a difference in their world. By doing so, they will not only enrich their work environment and inspire their colleagues, but they will also propel themselves at the forefront of academic originality.

Philippe Caignon,
Concordia University, French Studies

REFLECTION AND APPLICATION ACTIVITIES

The advice in this chapter outlines a number of pitfalls in the PhD journey that require confidence to overcome, as well as the negative consequences of not having enough confidence.

Some of the advice emphasizes the importance of not comparing yourself to others, staying true to yourself, and owning your project. Others remind us to avoid yet another trap: overconfidence.

Our activity Competence-Belief-Confidence Inventory invites you to explore the areas in which you feel confident, and areas in which you might be overconfident. Think of this as an opportunity to diagnose your confidence. We offer two concrete strategies to deepen confidence: Visualizing Success and Inspiring Your Best Self. Both activities can be used often throughout your PhD journey and beyond. If you decide you are overconfident in some areas, approach these activities with the goal of cultivating a healthier self-concept!

Activity 1: Competence-Belief-Confidence Inventory

Fill in the table below to gain a clearer understanding of the skills, abilities, and life aspects that you and others believe you are competent in, identifying evidence for these beliefs. Also use the chart to identify areas in which you might be over- or underconfident.

Based on the table above, what actions might you take to adjust any difference in how others perceive your confidence and how you perceive your confidence?

	Aspect/Area	Evidence
Aspects of my competence that I DO believe in		
Aspects of my competence that OTHERS believe in		
Areas I am underconfident in		
Areas I am overconfident in		

Activity 2: Visualizing Success

Just like a high-performance athlete or entrepreneur, visualizing success can help you develop and maintain a "winning" mindset. There are two ways to visualize success. One or both are impactful.

1. Recall a time when you felt really confident and performed well. In a quiet moment, perhaps before sleeping or upon waking, put yourself back in that moment of success. Remember how you felt, how you looked, your posture and facial expressions. How you interacted with others or your environment, what you said. Do all you can to relive the emotions that went with that moment of success. If you practice this recall, not only will it affect your mood every time, but during times of doubt or pressure you'll be able to invoke the feeling of confidence in the moment!

   Use the following guiding questions to recall the experience:

   a. *What was the context of the situation?*
   b. *Who was I with?*
   c. *What was I wearing?*
   d. *How did I prepare for the event?*
   e. *What did I do right before and after the event?*
   f. *What thoughts or meanings did I make of the event?*

   Do this exercise with a few past experiences. See if you notice patterns in your answers. Take note of these patterns – they will help you feel more confident in future events.

2. Just like an athlete visualizes their future performance, imagining in fine detail every movement of their body, you too can visualize a future event, and how you will perform with confidence. Such visualizations have a positive influence on actual performance. If you have an event coming up, take a moment to think about how you would like to perform during the event. You can use the same questions above to engage in visualizing what success will look like for you during this event. It can be helpful to narrate (write or speak) or draw this visualization.

Activity 3: Inspiring Your Best Self

Another strategy to help build confidence is to consider role models for our performance and behavior. The goal here is not to mimic our role models but rather to be inspired by them, and to let that inspiration give us confidence in our own expression of success.

In the table below, take a moment to list various people who inspire you in the left-hand column. These could be people in your field, family, or they could be people more removed; for example, performers, politicians, innovators, activists, etc. For example, you, like us, might be inspired by RuPaul or Oprah or a high school teacher. The point is that no one person will embody all the characteristics that inspire you; instead, you can learn from each person to inspire the best version of yourself.

Have as many as you like and imagine a picture of each of them. In the second column, jot down what specifically inspires you about them. It could be the way they give speeches, or the way they humanize interactions, or the way they communicate complex ideas simply, or the way they always show up with a positive attitude. The list is endless. Remember, the goal is not to find the perfect version of yourself in any of these people – that doesn't exist in someone else – but to find specific aspects of people's behaviors, skills, and knowledge that you find inspiring.

Role Model	What Inspires Me?

Once you have done this, look across your role models and the characteristics they represent. Now consider how you embody and enact these characteristics in your daily life and work. Do they represent strengths for you? Feel free to underline these traits and behaviors and take a moment to let these strengths bolster your confidence. Are other traits areas for growth and development? Feel free to circle them. Consider how you will develop your capacity in these areas. Carry your role models and their inspiration with you as you engage in new tasks and events in your PhD. Remind yourself of their strength and how they can inspire yours!

Activity 4: The Three Rs of Reflection

Recall: I Must Remember

What are my top takeaways from this chapter?

Revise: What Do I Want to Do Differently?

Based on the advice from this chapter, what is most important for me to personally change or improve? Write down a commitment for one small action you will do differently right away.

Reimagine: What Do I Hope Will Happen?

Reimagining a future reality for ourselves and setting clear intentions is powerful in changing our current practices and achieving our goals. Based on the advice from this chapter, describe a vision of yourself in the future. A prompt for this exercise: *In one year, I hope …*

CHAPTER NINE

Onward

Like a patchwork quilt, the advice throughout this book varies, with individual pieces sometimes vibrant, sometimes comforting, and sometimes starkly contrasting, yet all connected to themes resonant with the doctoral journey. Let's return to these themes once more to stitch together the big takeaway messages from this book. This concluding chapter is intended to help you see the big picture – the full quilt, to carry the metaphor forward – and to empower you to continue onward with confidence in your doctoral choices.

Make Wise Choices

The decisions you make during your PhD will shape your experience and outcomes, both within the PhD and beyond.

From choosing the right supervisor to selecting your research topic, each choice carries weight. As discussed in Chapter 2, making wise decisions involves careful consideration of your goals, the available evidence, and the advice of trusted mentors. Reflect on your assumptions, weigh the evidence, and seek advice to navigate the labyrinth of choices with confidence. Most importantly, remember that you are not alone in navigating these choices; if you foster and rely on positive relationships along the way, the journey will be easier. The following are the key takeaway messages from Chapter 2:

- A PhD is all about making choices – a good scholar learns how to academically defend their choices.
- Begin your PhD and choose your topic by asking these questions: What am I passionate about? What is important to study? Why am I the right person to study that topic?
- Your choice of supervisor is essential. Spend time investigating different supervisors, how they supervise, and the kind of PhD experience you will have with them.
- Throughout your PhD, know that you will need to make difficult choices about your academic direction, work assignments, conflict and how to resolve it, and future career paths. Talking with mentors, supervisors, peers, and family is useful in navigating these choices.

Foster Relationships

Relationships are the backbone of a fulfilling PhD journey. As highlighted in Chapter 3, fostering strong connections with supervisors, peers, family, and friends can provide support, motivation, and inspiration during the uphills and downhills of doctoral studies. These relationships not only help you weather the storms of your doctoral journey but also enrich your professional and personal life. Academia is a collaborative endeavor, and building a network of supportive relationships is crucial for your success. Key messages from Chapter 3 include the following:

- PhDs can look like lonely journeys, but they are not. Spend time identifying the various relationships that support you during this time, and those that you hope to cultivate.
- Relationships are not always easy. Conflicts arise. Navigating difficulty in relationships is part of the PhD journey. Look at these times as learning opportunities, and know that there are supports at the university, and in others (i.e., peers, mentors, and family), to help you work through conflict.
- The relationship with your supervisor is key to success. Take steps to ensure this relationship is set up for success. Learn about your supervisor. Prepare for meetings with your supervisor. If possible, plan for joint projects and collaborative work with your supervisor. Your supervisor may have a well-established practice of supervision; spend time discussing their supervision practice so that assumptions of how you should and will work together become transparent and explicit.

Manage Your Project

Managing your project is also a key ingredient for your success. Effective project management is essential for keeping your research and studies on track. Chapter 4 offers strategies for planning, risk management, continuous writing, and more. Use tools like Gantt charts to visualize your progress and stay organized. Review and update your plans regularly and be open to opportunities and change in the face of challenges. Continuous writing, even in small increments, will help you maintain momentum and reduce the burden of last-minute deadlines. Managing your project by being clear about your goals and guardrails will help you move forward with purpose and balance. Essential points from Chapter 4 include the following:

- Managing your dissertation project and degree completion is all about steady work and balance: finding *your* rhythm of structure and flexibility. For some this will involve a regular daily writing routine, for others this will involve deadline-based writing. Whatever your approach, make it explicit so that you can begin to trust your approach to work and your capacity to move forward with your goals.
- Writing is fundamental to progress in a PhD. While there are other modes of representation, and some dissertations take on other formats, writing, for many, remains the primary method of communicating ideas in academia. As such, developing your writing skills and habits is a requirement for you to not only make

progress, but enjoy the journey. Spend time, early on, figuring out how to write and cultivating positive and joyful writing habits. Too often this skill is not explicitly taught, talked about, or developed.

Seek Balance

Achieving balance is perhaps one of the most challenging aspects of the PhD journey. Chapter 5 emphasizes the importance of maintaining a healthy work-life balance. Balance is not just about managing time but also about maintaining your well-being. Integrating leisure activities, social interactions, and self-care into your routine is foundational to strong academic work. Recognize the importance of taking breaks, connecting with loved ones, and engaging in activities that bring you joy. Your work will benefit from it, perhaps more than you know. Chapter 5's takeaway messages include the following:

- The work and life habits formed during PhD studies often follow us into our careers. Developing positive work-life balance is challenging but essential for sustaining yourself during the marathon that is a PhD, and beyond.
- A focus on balance means paying attention to your physical, emotional, intellectual, and spiritual well-being, and purposefully engaging in activities that nourish each of these (and other) dimensions of yourself.

- Seeking balance also means setting boundaries – turning off your computer, saying "no" to a task, or setting your alarm to wake up early to engage in a few productive hours of work or exercise, for example. Boundaries require discipline; knowing what will enable or detract from our work and well-being, then acting in accordance with that knowledge.

Focus on What Matters

With the plethora of distractions in today's world, staying focused on what truly matters can be challenging, but it is essential, especially for the PhD student. Chapter 6 provides guidance on distinguishing between productive possibilities and destructive distractions. Set clear priorities for yourself, learn to say "no" when necessary, and stay true to your goals. Recognize that life events are as significant as your research (if not more so) and should be integrated into your journey, not brushed aside. Figuring out what matters most to you – and revisiting this from time to time – will help you make wise choices, keep you motivated, and ensure you use your PhD time to cultivate the foundations for a full and fabulous life. Key takeaway thoughts from Chapter 6 include the following:

- Take time to think and be curious; explore the many possibilities that a PhD affords, after all it is *your* degree and can lead you wherever you want! Understanding how your PhD connects with larger life goals will enable you to see what really matters to you.

- Learn how to say "yes" to the opportunities that excite you and that advance your goals, and "no" to the opportunities that don't. This is a life skill, so developing it now, in your PhD, is worthwhile.
- Identify specific experiences and relationships you want to have during your PhD – plan for them and make them happen. Cultivate the PhD experience you want to have.

Cultivate a Growth Mindset

Failures and setbacks are inevitable in any ambitious pursuit. Chapter 7 encourages you to adopt a growth mindset to tackle those difficult times by viewing challenges as opportunities for learning and development. Embrace failures as part of your growth and use them as stepping-stones to success. Cultivate resilience and persistence, knowing that your potential is not fixed but can be developed through mindset, effort, perseverance, and belief in yourself. Chapter 7 reminds us of the following:

- To accept obstacles as learning opportunities. In a PhD, obstacles and (negative) feedback are, at times, plentiful. If you have a fixed mindset toward these experiences, it will be difficult to find the motivation to move forward. If you see them as stepping-stones, you will move further, faster.
- Avoid comparisons, which is easier said than done. While academia seems to have a preoccupation with

comparing one scholar to another, try to recognize the strength of your own success trajectory – Where did you start from? What have you accomplished? And, where are you going next?
- Embrace feedback. Whether it is feedback from your supervisor, a journal reviewer, or your family member, feedback challenges us to think about our work and make choices about it. In essence, it helps us become more confident scholars by asking us to defend our academic choices and refine our arguments. Take instances of feedback seriously as professional opportunities to become a better scholar.

Believe in Yourself

Self-efficacy is one of the most powerful predictors of success. Chapter 8 discusses the importance of believing in your abilities and cultivating confidence. Your belief in yourself can influence how others perceive you and can drive you toward achieving your goals. Surround yourself with supportive people who believe in you and seek opportunities to boost your confidence. If you believe in yourself, others are more likely to believe in you too. The following points summarize our final advice chapter:

- We are always developing our confidence as scholars as we enter new and different arenas. For many, starting a PhD might come with a bout of imposter syndrome. For others, the opposite. Learning to assess and regulate your

confidence in relation to your abilities and the context you are in is a valuable skill. However, at base, you must believe in yourself and your capacity to achieve your goals.
- Your relationships – with your supervisor, peers, mentors, and family members – can help you assess and regulate your confidence, and when needed, give you a shot of confidence! Ask for their support in this area because research tells us that your self-efficacy and confidence are essential to your success.

As you engage with these themes, remember that variation in specific pieces of advice reflects the complexity of the doctoral journey, as well as life itself. There is no one-size-fits-all solution to any PhD challenge for a very good reason: every PhD student, every PhD project, and every PhD supervisor is different. Who you are determines the most feasible advice to follow. If any one piece of advice seems beyond your scope or does not fit with your personality and circumstance, take heart and acknowledge the importance of understanding yourself, identifying your goals, and caring for yourself in your own way. Selecting the advice that applies to you is an exercise in being your authentic self within the context of your doctoral work.

This exhortation holds broad implications for graduate students well beyond how you relate to this book, for who you are influences every aspect of your doctorate. Humans have an inextricable and undeniable effect on what they study, and that *fact* must be acknowledged as part of doctoral studies and supervision. Your ways of knowing and being shape your way of inquiring and representing knowledge.

Moving toward clarity on who you are and what your goals are becomes particularly important when facing pressure in your doctoral program to conform. Consider, for example, that students often select their supervisors based on their deep knowledge of and stature in a field. It is only natural to be inspired by and aspire to become like one's supervisor. Inversely, supervisors tend to train students in the ways that they were trained, reinforcing a mini-me approach to graduate supervision.

In the forward to Robert Nash's[1] text *Liberating Scholarly Writing,* Carol Witherell notes that we teach and learn who we are and who we might become. As you select the advice in this book that is most relevant to you, lean into your uniqueness in your scholarly work. Doing so will ensure what you contribute through your doctoral studies reflects your passions and perspectives. YOU are the author of your dissertation. While it is true that we might stand on the shoulders of our supervisors, we do not need to stand in their image too. As Oscar Wilde would say, *be yourself, your supervisor is already taken*. Bold academics forge new paths of inquiry and dare to express knowledge in new ways.

As we conclude, it's no accident that the seven themes in this book resonate with all doctoral journeys. The contributions of these top supervisors from around the globe provide a guide, offering wisdom and support through every stage of your PhD journey. It is now up to you to chart your path with intention, perseverance, and confidence. The world awaits your contributions. Journey onward.

A FINAL EXERCISE

In this final Three Rs of Reflection, we ask you to consider your top takeaways from this book, what you plan to do differently, and what your future reality looks like. We suggest using this exercise every four to six months to ensure you continue on an intentional path.

Recall: I Must Remember

What are my top takeaways from this book?

Revise: What Do I Want to Do Differently?

Based on this book, what is most important for me to personally change or improve? Write down a plan for how you want to move forward with your PhD studies at this point. We encourage you to revisit this plan every four to six months.

Reimagine: What Do I Hope Will Happen?

Reimagining a future reality for ourselves and setting clear intentions is powerful in changing our current practices and achieving our goals. Based on the advice you have read in this book, describe a vision of yourself in the future. A prompt for this exercise: *In one year, I hope …*

Appendix: Further Reading

While *The Prosperous PhD* offers guidance across many aspects of doctoral study, no single resource can address every unique experience or challenge that students may encounter. To support readers in exploring topics beyond the scope of this book, we have compiled a selection of additional resources that offer specialized advice on academic career planning, research project management, mental well-being, and scholarly writing. These readings provide valuable perspectives and strategies to complement and deepen the insights shared within these pages.

Belcher, W.L. (2019). *Writing your journal article in twelve weeks: A guide to academic publishing success*. University of Chicago Press.

A practical resource for PhD students aiming to publish during their programs. It offers a step-by-step approach to academic writing and publishing.

Calarco, J.M. (2020). *A field guide to grad school: Uncovering the hidden curriculum*. Princeton University Press.

Demystifies the unwritten norms of graduate school, offering practical insights into advisor relationships, publishing, and overall success.

Kelsky, K. (2015). *The professor is in: The essential guide to turning your PhD into a job*. Crown Publishing Group.

Candid advice on navigating the academic job market, covering everything from CVs to interviews for both academic and industry careers.

Lee, A. (2020). *Successful research projects: A guide for postgraduates.* Routledge.

Step-by-step advice for managing research projects, from planning to publication, helping students stay organized and on schedule.

Mewburn, I. (2019). *Becoming an academic: How to get through grad school and beyond*. Johns Hopkins University Press.

Strategies for PhD students transitioning to academic careers, with tips on publishing, networking, and time management.

Mewburn, I. (2021–). *The thesis whisperer*. https://thesiswhisperer.com/

Advice on thesis writing and PhD life, with support for both practical and mental health challenges.

Mewburn, I., Firth, K., & Lehmann, S. (2018). *How to fix your academic writing trouble: A practical guide*. Open University Press.

A guide to overcoming writing challenges, this book provides exercises and advice for clarity, focus, and productivity in academic writing.

Phillips, E., and Johnson, C. (2022). *How to get a PhD: A handbook for students and their supervisors*. 7th ed. Open University Press.

Strategies for students and supervisors to navigate the challenges of PhD study and build productive working relationships.

Rugg, G., & Petre, M. (2020). *The unwritten rules of PhD research*. 3rd ed. Open University Press.

Discusses the "unwritten rules" of research success, covering topics like academic expectations, focus, and navigating academic culture.

Notes

1. Beginning: The Doctoral Journey

1 Dore, R. (1997). *The diploma disease: Education, qualification and development* (2nd ed.). Institute of Education, University of London.

2 Charles, C.H., & Øverlid, V. (2020, July 3). Tuition hikes exacerbating existing challenges for international students. *Policy Options*. https://policyoptions.irpp.org/magazines/july-2020/tuition-hikes-exacerbating-existing- challenges-for-international-students/

3 Hazell, C.M., Chapman, L., Valeix, S.F., Roberts, P., Niven, J.E., & Berry, C. (2020). Understanding the mental health of doctoral researchers: A mixed methods systematic review with meta-analysis and meta-synthesis. *Systematic Reviews*, *9*(1), 1–30. https://doi.org/10.1186/s13643-020-01443-1

4 Laufer, M., & Gorup, M. (2019). The invisible others: Stories of international doctoral student dropout. *Higher Education*, *78*(1), 165–181. https://doi.org/10.1007/s10734-018-0337-z

5 Mackie, S.A., & Bates, G.W. (2019). Contribution of the doctoral education environment to PhD candidates' mental health problems: A scoping review. *Higher Education Research & Development*, *38*(3), 565–578. https://doi.org/10.1080/07294360.2018.1556620

6 Evans, T.M., Bira, L., Gastelum, J.B., Weiss, L.T., & Vanderford, N.L. (2018). Evidence for a mental health crisis in graduate education. *Nature Biotechnology*, *36*(3), 282–284. https://doi.org/10.1038/nbt.4089

7 Panger, G., Tryon, J., & Smith, A. (2014). *Graduate student happiness & well-being report*. The Graduate Assembly of the University of California, Berkeley. https://gradresources.org/wp-content/uploads/2015/09/wellbeingreport_2014-17.pdf

8 Smith, E., & Brooks, Z. (2015). *Graduate student mental health 2015*. National Association of Graduate-Professional Students, University of Arizona. http://nagps.org/wordpress/wp-content/uploads/2015/06/NAGPS_Institute_mental_health_survey_report_2015.pdf

9 Hazell et al. (2020).

10 Levecque, K., Anseel, F., De Beuckelaer, A., Van der Heyden, J., & Gisle, L. (2017). Work organization and mental health problems in PhD students. *Research Policy*, *46*(4), 868–879. https://doi.org/10.1016/j.respol.2017.02.008

11 Litalien, D., & Guay, F. (2015). Dropout intentions in PhD studies: A comprehensive model based on interpersonal relationships and motivational resources. *Contemporary Educational Psychology*, *41*, 218–231. https://doi.org/10.1016/j.cedpsych.2015.03.004

12 Mackie & Bates (2019).

13 Sverdlik, A., & Hall, N.C. (2020). Not just a phase: Exploring the role of program stage on well-being and motivation in doctoral students. *Journal of Adult and Continuing Education*, *26*(1), 97–124. https://doi.org/10.1177/1477971419842887

14 Panger, Tryon, & Smith (2014).

15 Cardilini, A.P.A., Risely, A., & Richardson, M.F. (2022). Supervising the PhD: Identifying common mismatches in expectations between candidate and supervisor to improve research training outcomes. *Higher Education Research & Development*. https://doi.org/10.1080/07294360.2021.1874887

16 Janssen, S., van Vuuren, M., & de Jong, M.D.T. (2021). Sensemaking in supervisor-doctoral student relationships: Revealing schemas on the fulfillment of basic psychological needs. *Studies in Higher Education*, *46*(12), 2738–2750. https://doi.org/10.1080/03075079.2020.1804850

17 Parker-Jenkins, M. (2018). Mind the gap: Developing the roles, expectations and boundaries in the doctoral supervisor–supervisee relationship. *Studies in Higher Education*, *43*(1), 57–71. https://doi.org/10.1080/03075079.2016.1153622

18 Parker-Jenkins (2018).

19 Canolle, F., & Vinot, D. (2021). What is your PhD worth? The value of a PhD for finding employment outside of academia. *European Management Review*, *18*(2), 157–171. https://doi.org/10.1111/emre.12445

20 Cardoso, S., Santos, S., Diogo, S., Soares, D., & Carvalho, T. (2022). The transformation of doctoral education: A systematic literature review. *Higher Education*, *84*(4), 885–908. https://doi.org/10.1007/s10734-021-00805-5

21 Seo, G., Ahn, J., Huang, W.-H., Makela, J.P., & Yeo, H.J.T. (2021). Pursuing careers inside or outside academia? Factors associated with doctoral students' career decision making. *Journal of Career Development*, *48*(6), 957–972. https://doi.org/10.1177/0894845320907968

2. Make Wise Choices

1 Kahneman, D. (2013). *Thinking, fast and slow*. Farrar, Straus and Giroux.
2 Weiss, C.H. (1980). Knowledge creep and decision accretion. *Knowledge: Creation, Diffusion, Utilization, 1*(3), 381–404.
3 Cain, T., Brindley, S., Brown, C., Jones, G., & Riga, F. (2019). Bounded decision-making, teachers' reflection and organisational learning: How research can inform teachers and teaching. *British Educational Research Journal, 45*(5), 1072–1087. https://doi.org/10.1002/berj.3551
4 McAlpine, L., & Emmioğlu, E. (2015). Navigating careers: Perceptions of sciences doctoral students, post-PhD researchers and pre-tenure academics. *Studies in Higher Education, 40*(10), 1770–1785. https://doi.org/10.1080/03075079.2014.914908
5 Bersola, S.H., Stolzenberg, E.B., Love, J., & Fosnacht, K. (2014). Understanding admitted doctoral students' institutional choices: Student experiences versus faculty and staff perceptions. *American Journal of Education, 120*(4), 515–543. https://doi.org/10.1086/676923
6 Gladwell, M. (2011, February 6). The order of things. *The New Yorker*. www.newyorker.com/magazine/2011/02/14/the-order-of-things
7 Nutley, S.M., Walter, I., & Davies, H.T.O. (2007). *Using evidence: How research can inform public services*. Policy Press.
8 Hoekstra, F., Mrklas, K.J., Khan, M., McKay, R.C., Vis-Dunbar, M., Sibley, K.M., Nguyen, T., Graham, I.D., SCI Guiding Principles Consensus Panel, & Gainforth, H.L. (2020). A review of reviews on principles, strategies, outcomes and impacts of research partnerships approaches: A first step in synthesising the research partnership literature. *Health Research Policy & Systems, 18*, 1–23. https://doi.org/10.1186/s12961-020-0544-9
9 Zhao, C.-M., Golde, C.M., & McCormick, A.C. (2007). More than a signature: How advisor choice and advisor behaviour affect doctoral student satisfaction. *Journal of Further and Higher Education, 31*(3), 263–281. https://doi.org/10.1080/03098770701424983
10 Denis, C., Colet, N.R., & Lison, C. (2019). Doctoral supervision in North America: Perception and challenges of supervisor and supervisee. *Higher Education Studies, 9*(1), 30–39. https://doi.org/10.5539/hes.v9n1p30
11 Janssen, S., van Vuuren, M., & de Jong, M.D.T. (2021). Sensemaking in supervisor-doctoral student relationships: Revealing schemas on the fulfillment of basic psychological needs. *Studies in Higher Education, 46*(12), 2738–2750. https://doi.org/10.1080/03075079.2020.1804850
12 Sverdlik, A., & Hall, N.C. (2019). Not just a phase: Exploring the role of program stage on well-being and motivation in doctoral students. *Journal of Adult and Continuing Education, 26*(1), 97–124. https://doi.org/10.1177/1477971419842887
13 Cain, T., Brindley, S., Brown, C., Jones, G., & Riga, F. (2019). Bounded decision-making, teachers' reflection and organisational learning: How research can inform teachers and teaching. *British Educational Research Journal, 45*(5), 1072–1087. https://doi.org/10.1002/berj.3551

3. Foster Relationships

1 Mineo, L. (2017, April 11). Good genes are nice, but joy is better. *The Harvard Gazette*. https://news.harvard.edu/gazette/story/2017/04/over-nearly-80-years-harvard-study-has-been-showing-how-to-live-a-healthy-and-happy-life/
2 Brook, J., Catlin, S., DeLuca, C., Doe, C., Huntly, A., & Searle, M. (2010). Conceptions of doctoral education: The PhD as pathmaking. *Reflective Practice, 11*(5), 657–668.
3 Bakhtin, M.M. (1981). Discourse in the novel. In M. Holoquist (Ed.), *The dialogic imagination* (pp. 259–422, p. 294). University of Austin Press.

4. Manage Your Project

1 Backlund, F. (2017). A project perspective on doctoral studies – a student point of view. *International Journal of Educational Management, 31*(7), 908–921. https://doi.org/10.1108/IJEM-04-2016-0075
2 Mirzaei, M., & Mabin, V.J. (2013). The PhD in light of project management. *Proceedings of the 47th Annual Conference of the ORSNZ, 81*, 1–10. https://doi.org/ 10.13140/RG.2.1.4916.4562
3 Berg, M., & Seeber, B.K. (2016). *The slow professor: Challenging the culture of speed in the academy*. University of Toronto Press.
4 Lamott, A. (2005). Shitty first drafts. In P. Eschholz, A. Rosa, & V. Clark (Eds.), *Language awareness: Readings for college writers* (9th ed., pp. 93–96). Bedford/St. Martin's.

5. Seek Balance

1 Headlee, C. (2021). *Do nothing: How to break away from overworking, overdoing, and underliving*. Harmony Books.
2 Sverdlik, A., Hall, N.C., McAlpine, L., & Hubbard, K. (2018). The PhD experience: A review of the factors influencing doctoral students' completion, achievement, and well-being. *International Journal of Doctoral Studies, 13*, 361–388.
3 Sverdlik et al. (2018).
4 Levecque, K., Anseel, F., De Beuckelaer, A., Van der Heyden, J., & Gisle, L. (2017). Work organization and mental health problems in PhD students. *Research Policy, 46*(4), 868–879.
5 Panger, G., Tryon, J., & Smith, A. (2014). *Graduate student happiness & well-being report*. The Graduate Assembly of the University of California, Berkeley. https://gradresources.org/wp-content/uploads/2015/09/wellbeingreport_2014-17.pdf
6 Castelló, M., Pardo, M., Sala-Bubaré, A., & Suñe-Soler, N. (2017). Why do students consider dropping out of doctoral degrees? Institutional and personal factors. *Higher Education, 74*, 1053–1068.

7 Clear, J. (2018). *Atomic habits: An easy and proven way to build good habits and break bad ones*. Avery.
8 Clear (2018).
9 A German word referring to a relationship that is meaningful and significant for a particular chapter of life. See Stefan Rinke's other piece of advice in Chapter 6.

6. Focus on What Matters

1 Ducharme, J. (2023, August 10). Why everyone's worried about their attention span – and how to improve yours. *Time*. https://time.com/6302294/why-you-cant-focus-anymore-and-what-to-do-about-it/
2 Zahariades, D. (2017). *The art of saying no: How to stand your ground, reclaim your time and energy, and refuse to be taken for granted (without feeling guilty!)*. Independently published.
3 Zahariades (2017).

7. Cultivate a Growth Mindset

1 Sverdlik, A., Hall, N.C., McAlpine, L., & Hubbard, K. (2018). The PhD experience: A review of the factors influencing doctoral students' completion, achievement, and well-being. *International Journal of Doctoral Studies*, *13*, 361–388.
2 Dweck, C.S. (2006). *Mindset: The new psychology of success*. Random House.
3 Limeri, L.B., Carter, N.T., Choe, J., Harper, H.G., Martin, H.R., Benton, A., & Dolan, E.L. (2020). Growing a growth mindset: Characterizing how and why undergraduate students' mindsets change. *International Journal of STEM Education*, *7*. https://doi.org/10.1186/s40594-020-00227-2
4 Aditomo, A. (2015). Students' response to academic setback: "Growth mindset" as a buffer against demotivation. *International Journal of Educational Psychology*, 4(2), 198–222. https://doi.org/10.17583/ijep.2015.1482
5 Burnette, J.L., Knouse, L.E., Vavra, D.T., O'Boyle, E., & Brooks, M.A. (2020). Growth mindsets and psychological distress: A meta-analysis. *Clinical Psychology Review*, *77*, 101816.
6 Dweck (2006).
7 Yeager, D.S., Hanselman, P., & Walton, G.M. et al. (2019). A national experiment reveals where a growth mindset improves achievement. *Nature*, *573*, 364–369.
8 Dweck, C.S., Walton, G.M., & Cohen, G.L. (2014). *Academic tenacity: Mindsets and skills that promote long-term learning*. Bill and Melinda Gates Foundation.
9 Yeager et al. (2019).

8. Believe in Yourself

1 Bandura, A. (1977). Self-efficacy: Toward a unifying theory of behavioral change. *Psychological Review, 84*(2), 191–215. https://doi.org/10.1037//0033-295x.84.2.191

2 Bandura, A. (1982). Self-efficacy mechanism in human agency. *American Psychologist, 37*(2), 122–147. https://doi.org/10.1037/0003-066X.37.2.122

3 Stajkovic, A.D., & Luthans, F. (1998). Self-efficacy and work-related performance: A meta-analysis. *Psychological Bulletin, 124*(2), 240–261.

4 Taylor, M.S., Locke, E.A., Lee, C., & Gist, M.E. (1984). Type A behavior and faculty research productivity: What are the mechanisms? *Organizational Behavior and Human Performance, 34*(3), 402–418. https://doi.org/10.1016/0030-5073(84)90046-1

5 Bouffard-Bouchard, T. (1990). Influence of self-efficacy on performance in a cognitive task. *The Journal of Social Psychology, 130*(3), 353–363. https://doi.org/10.1080/00224545.1990.9924591

6 Dogan, U. (2015). Student engagement, academic self-efficacy, and academic motivation as predictors of academic performance. *The Anthropologist, 20*(3), 553–561. https://doi.org/10.1080/09720073.2015.11891759

7 Schönfeld, P., Brailovskaia, J., Bieda, A., Chi Zhang, X., & Margraf, J. (2016). The effects of daily stress on positive and negative mental health: Mediation through self-efficacy. *International Journal of Clinical and Health Psychology, 16*(1), 1–10. https://doi.org/10.1016/j.ijchp.2015.08.005

8 Juth, V., Smyth, J.M., & Santuzzi, A.M. (2008). How do you feel? Self-esteem predicts affect, stress, social interaction, and symptom severity during daily life in patients with chronic illness. *Journal of Health Psychology, 13*(7), 884–894. https://doi.org/ 10.1177/1359105308095062

9 O'Leary, A. (1985). Self-efficacy and health. *Behaviour Research and Therapy, 23*(4), 437–451. https://doi.org/10.1016/0005-7967(85)90172-X

10 Elshatarat, R.A., Yacoub, M.I., Khraim, F.M., Saleh, Z.T., & Afaneh, T.R. (2016). Self-efficacy in treating tobacco use: A review article. *Proceedings of Singapore Healthcare, 25*(4), 243–248. https://doi.org/10.1177/2010105816667137

11 Bandura, A. (1997). *Self-efficacy: The exercise of control.* Freeman.

12 Wearing, J. (2021). Attributes and behaviours of teachers supporting student creativity in secondary school. In K. Walker, B. Kutsyuruba, & S. Cherkowski (Eds.), *Positive leadership for flourishing schools* (pp. 267–282). Information Age Publishing.

13 Goldsmith, B. (2010). *100 ways to boost your self-confidence: Believe in yourself and others will too.* Career Press.

14 Madon, S., Willard, J., Guyll, M., & Scherr, K.C. (2011). Self-fulfilling prophecies: Mechanisms, power, and links to social problems. *Social and Personality Psychology Compass, 5*(8), 578–590.

15 Jordan, K., Zajac, R., Bernstein, D., Joshi, C., & Garry, M. (2022). Trivially informative semantic context inflates people's confidence they can perform a highly complex skill. *Royal Society Open Science, 9*(3), 211977.

16 Kruger, J., & Dunning, D. (1999). Unskilled and unaware of it: How difficulties in recognizing one's own incompetence lead to inflated self-assessments. *Journal of Personality and Social Psychology*, *77*(6), 1121–1134.

17 Johnson, D.D.P., & Fowler, J.H. (2011). The evolution of overconfidence. *Nature*, *477*, 317–320.

9. Onward

1 Nash, R.J. (2004). *Liberating scholarly writing: The power of personal narrative*. Teachers College Press.

Contributors

Authors

JUDY WEARING, Lead Learning Architect, Canada

Dr. Judy Wearing is an educator, author, and PhD coach currently working as a Lead Learning Architect creating educational programs for the healthcare industry. She has two PhDs, one involving experimental research in evolutionary biology from the University of Oxford, the other a qualitative study in education from Queen's University. Her research has focused on encouraging and discouraging creativity in education settings. She has written over twenty nonfiction books for adults and children including *Edison's Concrete Piano* (ECW Press, 2009) and her upcoming title *Anxious and Hairy*. Her diverse activities are connected by endless fascination with human nature and a desire to make a positive impact on others' lives.

CHRISTOPHER DELUCA, Queen's University, Canada

Dr. Christopher DeLuca is a professor of education in the Faculty of Education and former Associate Dean at the School of Graduate Studies and Postdoctoral Affairs, Queen's University (Kingston, Canada). His research examines the intersection of assessment, curriculum, and pedagogy from sociocultural frameworks. His work largely focuses on supporting teachers in negotiating these critical areas of practice to enhance student learning for all. He has published over 125 manuscripts and has received numerous awards for his research, teaching, and supervision. Chris has worked extensively with graduate students as a supervisor, committee member, and examiner, nationally and internationally. In his current role, he works with graduate students across the Queen's campus as they navigate the PhD journey, often to overcome challenges and achieve success.

STEPHEN MACGREGOR, University of Calgary, Canada

Dr. Stephen MacGregor is an assistant professor of educational leadership, policy, and governance at the University of Calgary's Werklund School of Education. Presently, he focuses on three interrelated strands of inquiry: (1) the relational networks among universities and secondary and elementary schools; (2) the influence of positive school leadership on the mobilization of research-informed teaching practices; and (3) the mechanisms and impacts of coproduction as one approach to knowledge mobilization. He is also a recent PhD graduate and has been instrumental in "testing" the advice for its value to the lived experiences of PhD students. He continues to support graduate students directly through his supervision but also as the representative to the New Scholar Advisory Board for the Canadian Educational Researchers' Association and a network coordinator for the International Congress for School Effectiveness and Improvement.

Advice Contributors

JULIA N. ALBRECHT, University of Otago, New Zealand

Dr. Julia N. Albrecht is an associate professor in the Department of Tourism in the Otago Business School, University of Otago, New Zealand. Her research and publication record features works on destination management for sustainability, tourism strategy, and visitor management. Julia won the University of Otago Supervisor of the Year Award in 2023 and the Otago Business School Supervisor of the Year Award in 2022 and 2023.

EMMA ALLEN-VERCOE, University of Guelph, Canada

I am a professor and Tier 1 Canada Research Chair at the University of Guelph, Canada, though I'm originally from the UK and started my career there. I study the microbial ecology of the human gut, earning myself the unofficial title of "Professor Poo." Projects in my very busy research lab span many different areas, including the study of diseases such as colorectal cancer and diabetes, as well as working with Indigenous peoples to uncover "missing microbes" of the gut microbiome that have been lost during the process of industrialization.

RICHARD ASCOUGH, Queen's University, Canada

Richard Ascough is a professor in the School of Religion at Queen's University in Kingston, Canada. His research focuses on the formation of early Christian groups and Greco-Roman religious culture. He has published widely in the field with more than fifty articles and essays and ten books. He has also been recognized for his innovative and effective teaching in a number of ways, including the two top teaching awards at Queen's University and most recently the 3M National Teaching Fellowship.

EDWARD BALLEISEN, Duke University, United States

Edward J. Balleisen is Vice Provost for Interdisciplinary Studies at Duke, as well as professor of history and public policy. A graduate of Princeton and Yale, Balleisen has written widely on the historical intersections among law, business, and policy in the United States, as well as the evolution of American regulatory institutions and contemporary debates on regulatory governance. His most recent book is *Fraud: An American History from Barnum to Madoff* (2017). Balleisen has won two undergraduate teaching awards at Duke and the Graduate School Dean's Award for Excellence in Mentoring.

CHARLES BECKER, Duke University, United States

Charles Becker (BA, Grinnell; PhD, Princeton) joined Duke in 2003, where he directed the American Economic Association's Summer Program and Minority Scholarship Program (2003–7). Becker previously taught at University of Colorado Denver, Vanderbilt, and University of Colorado Boulder. In 2007, he was recognized as a lifetime member of the American Economic Association (AEA) for service to the profession; in 2019 he received the AEA's Committee on the Status of Minority Groups in the Economics Profession's mentorship award. He received Duke's equity, inclusion, and diversity award in 2008 and graduate faculty mentoring award in 2014.

MARK BELLGROVE, Monash University, Australia

Mark Bellgrove is Deputy Head of School (Research) and a professor in cognitive neuroscience in the School of Psychological Sciences at Monash University. He is also co-chair of Monash Neuroscience, a university-wide collective of over six hundred neuroscience researchers. At Monash Professor Bellgrove leads a multidisciplinary team studying the biological basis of attention and cognitive control in both health and disorder (ADHD, autism, stroke). In 2021, he was recognized as Supervisor of the Year within the Faculty of Medicine, Nursing and Health Sciences at Monash University. In 2023, he was awarded the Vice Chancellor's Prize for Research Engagement and Impact.

BARBARA A. BIESECKER, University of Georgia, United States

Barbara A. Biesecker is professor in the Department of Communication Studies at the University of Georgia. She has been the recipient of multiple teaching and mentoring awards, including the John I. Sisco Excellence in Teaching Award (2011), the Francine Merritt Award for Outstanding Contributions to the Lives of Women in Communication (2013), the UGA Graduate School's Outstanding Mentoring Award in the Humanities and Fine/Applied Arts (2015), and the NCA Rhetorical and Communication Theory Division's Faculty Mentorship Award (2015). In 2019, the National Communication Association's Teachers on Teaching division convened a "Spotlight Honoring Dr. Biesecker" at its annual convention.

KIM BROOKS, Dalhousie University, Canada

Kim Brooks is President and Vice-Chancellor at Dalhousie University and a 3M Fellow.

MARSHA BRYANT, University of Florida, United States

Marsha Bryant is professor of English and Distinguished Teaching Scholar at the University of Florida. Her interdisciplinary research links literature to advertising, art, magazines, and movies. She wrote the books *Women's Poetry and Popular Culture* and *Auden and Documentary in the 1930s*, and edited *Photo-Textualities: Reading Photographs and Literature*. Her recent essays appear in *Humanities*, *The Bloomsbury Handbook to Sylvia Plath*, and *The Massachusetts Review*. Bryant received a UF Doctoral Mentoring Award in 2018, and she served as her department's Director of Graduate Student Teaching from 2016 to 2019.

PHILIPPE CAIGNON, Concordia University, Canada

Philippe Caignon is the Associate Dean of Student Academic Services within the Faculty of Arts and Science at Concordia University. In 2007, Philippe received the Arts and Science Dean's Award for Excellence in Teaching. In 2014, he was awarded a 3M National Teaching Fellowship from the Society for Teaching and Learning in Higher Education, received the President's Excellence in Teaching Award from Concordia University, and was inducted to the Provost's Circle of Distinction. In 2017, he was the recipient of the Concordia University Alumni Award for Excellence in Teaching.

SARAH CARR, University of Otago, New Zealand

Dr. Sarah Carr has been the Director of the Doctor of Business Administration (DBA) degree at the University of Otago Business School since 2019. She has a background in quality assurance in higher education. Her research interests include doctoral supervision, student engagement and learning outcomes, and international student transitions. Prior to working at the University of Otago, Sarah was involved in international education at both the University of Queensland in Australia, and the University of Hertfordshire in the UK. She has degrees in history from Trent University, Canada; Durham University, UK; and the University of Otago, New Zealand.

MIRNA CARRANZA, McMaster University, Canada

Dr. Carranza is a professor in the School of Social Work, McMaster University. Experimenting with new forms of knowledge mobilization, the popular theater production of *We Are Not the Others* has brought the stories of women immigrants to new audiences to demystify the stories of migration often told in the news. She is the principal investigator of various international research projects: (i) "The Colonial Contours of Indigenous Women's Inclusion in the Americas – The Peruvian Experience"; (ii) "Evaluation of New Scenarios of Social and Gender Violence Faced by Lesbians and Bisexual Women, Exacerbated by the Context of Reduction of Rights in El Salvador"; (iii) "Borderless Violence: Central American Women at Home and the Diaspora in Canada." Her research work is informed by the coloniality of power as a way to strengthen methodological standpoints that contribute to a growing body of scholarship on community-based research as a process of decolonization, Indigenous methods, and horizontal global South/North dialogues, especially in social work.

YOLANDE E. CHAN, McGill University, Canada

Yolande E. Chan is Dean and James McGill Professor in the Desautels Faculty of Management at McGill University. Previously she served as Associate Dean (Research and PhD-MSc Programs) and E. Marie Shantz Chair of Digital Technology in the Smith School of Business at Queen's University. She holds a PhD in business administration from Western University, an MPhil in management studies from Oxford University, and SM and SB degrees in electrical engineering and computer science from MIT. She is a Rhodes Scholar. Yolande studies digital strategy, entrepreneurship, and innovation, and publishes in top journals. She is a Fellow, LEO Award winner, and Distinguished Cum Laude member of the Association for Information Systems and a recipient of several research and teaching awards, including the Queen's Award for Excellence in Graduate Supervision.

BRIAN CHEN, McGill University, Canada

Dr. Brian Chen is a professor at McGill University in the Departments of Medicine and Neurology & Neurosurgery. Dr. Chen's research seeks to understand how the instructions to wire up a brain are encoded within the genome. This research will also help provide insight into how these instructions can malfunction in mental disorders. In 2009, he was awarded the Canada Research Chair in Neural Circuit Formation, an Alfred P. Sloan Foundation Research Fellowship in 2011, and the Canadian Association for Neuroscience Young Investigator Award in 2014.

BRIAN P. COPPOLA, University of Michigan, United States

Dr. Brian P. Coppola (PhD, 1986, University of Wisconsin–Madison) is an Arthur F. Thurnau Professor of Chemistry at the University of Michigan, where he also served as the department's first Associate Chair for Educational Development & Practice. An organic chemist by training, his award-winning career contributed some of the earliest arguments for recognizing discipline-centered educational development and research as an area of specialization in higher education. His program for future faculty education, which has been institutionalized by his department, is built upon integrating an approach to scholarly development in education that parallels the familiar programs used in research.

TIM COULSON, University of Oxford, England

In 1994 when I was awarded my PhD, one of my advisors described it as the second-worst thesis ever produced, just behind his own. The only way was up! But I never had a plan; it was all luck. I was fortunate enough to get a postdoc at the Institute of Zoology in London, before spending time at Cambridge, Imperial College London, and Oxford. Along the way I applied for non-academic jobs, but failed to get positions as a weatherman on the TV, or as a civil servant. Academia really was the only option for me. I have always been inquisitive and imaginative, and I think it is those two characteristics, as well as lack of a plan, that helped my journey to where I am now.

JERRY DAVIS, University of Michigan, United States

Jerry Davis received his PhD from the Graduate School of Business at Stanford University and taught at Northwestern and Columbia before moving to the University of Michigan, where he is Associate Dean for Business+Impact, the Gilbert and Ruth Whitaker Professor of Business Administration, and professor of sociology. He previously served as editor-in-chief of the *Administrative Science Quarterly*. He has published widely in management, sociology, and finance. Books include *Social Movements and Organization Theory*; *Organizations and Organizing*; *Managed by the Markets: How Finance Reshaped America*; *Changing Your Company from the Inside Out: A Guide for Social Intrapreneurs*; and *The Vanishing American Corporation*. Davis's research is broadly concerned with the effects of finance on society, changes in the corporate economy, and new forms of organization.

PENNY EDGELL, University of Minnesota, United States

Penny Edgell (PhD, University of Chicago) is a Distinguished University Teaching Professor of sociology at the University of Minnesota. She studies contemporary American religion and nonreligion. Her research on congregational culture and institutional models appears in *Congregations in Conflict* (Cambridge University Press, 1999) and *Religion and Family in a Changing Society* (Princeton University Press, 2005). She analyzes religious influences on symbolic boundaries and social exclusion in *Religion Is Raced* (New York University Press, 2020), coedited with Grace Yukich, and in articles in the *American Sociological Review, Social Forces, Social Problems, Journal for the Scientific Study of Religion, Annual Review of Sociology*, and other outlets.

RICH EISENBERG, University of Rochester, United States

Richard (Rich) Eisenberg is the Tracy Harris Professor Emeritus at the University of Rochester. He has mentored more than eighty graduate and postdoctoral research students. During his more than fifty-year career, he has done groundbreaking work in solar photochemistry on energy conversion and in inorganic and organometallic chemistry on bond activation and catalysis. He has been a leader in the science community; a tireless advocate for global decarbonization; the editor of *Inorganic Chemistry*; associate editor of *PNAS*; and an innovative mentor of students from freshman to postdoc. He has served on numerous advisory boards and chaired a government committee that reviewed all higher degree chemistry programs in Israel.

MARK ELGAR, University of Melbourne, Australia

Professor Mark Elgar is an evolutionary ecologist with a PhD from the University of Cambridge. He held a SERC Fellowship at the University of Oxford and a QEII Fellowship at the University of NSW before joining the University of Melbourne. The unusually diverse projects undertaken in his research group reflect his supervising philosophy, which is recognized by national and university awards. In addition to publishing extensively within the scientific literature, he contributes to public debate through the traditional media and public events. Some of his commentary is informed by his role as a Research Integrity Advisor at the University of Melbourne.

RICHARD FULLER, University of Queensland, Australia

Richard Fuller is a professor at the University of Queensland. He studies how people have affected the natural world around them, and how some of their destructive effects can best be reversed. To answer these questions, the lab group works on pure and applied topics in biodiversity and conservation, spanning the fields of migration ecology, conservation planning, and urban ecology. Much of the work is interdisciplinary, focusing on the interactions between people and nature, how these can be enhanced, and how these relationships can be shaped to converge on coherent solutions to the biodiversity crisis. See https://www.fullerlab.org.

GILES GASPER, Durham University, England

Educated at the University of Oxford and the Pontifical Institute of Mediaeval Studies, Toronto, and appointed to Durham University, in the northeast of England, in 2004, Professor Giles Gasper is a medieval historian and theologian, with interests in the history of science, religious life, and food culture. He works collaboratively with many different fields and disciplines, directing the Ordered Universe project, which brings together natural scientists, social scientists, and medievalists to work on new editions, translations, and analyses of medieval science; and a new initiative from Durham Heritage360: Transformative Interdisciplinary Approaches to Natural and Cultural Heritage, an interdisciplinary and inter-sector project integrating the meaning and narrative assigned to heritage objects, locations, and landscapes, with understanding of their physical and ecological composition and attendant implications for heritage management. And on medieval food he gets to try out research in action at Blackfriars Restaurant in Newcastle upon Tyne.

THIERRY GIASSON, Université Laval, Canada

Thierry Giasson is a professor of political science at Université Laval, in Québec City, Canada. His research focuses on political journalism, political use of digital technologies, as well as political marketing strategies during elections. He is an award-winning teacher and the coeditor of the series Communication, Strategy and Politics at UBC Press. His work has been published in the *Canadian Journal of Political Science*, *Internet Policy Review*, *Journal of Information Technology and Politics*, and *Journal of Public Affairs*, among others.

FATMA MÜGE GÖÇEK, University of Michigan, United States

Fatma Müge Göçek is a professor of sociology at the University of Michigan, Ann Arbor. Her research focuses on the comparative analysis of history, politics, gender, and collective violence from a critical, DuBoisian perspective. Her sole-authored works include *East Encounters West* (Oxford University Press, 1987); *Rise of the Bourgeoisie, Demise of Empire: Ottoman Westernization and Social Change* (Oxford University Press, 1996); *The Transformation of Turkey* (I.B. Tauris, 2011); and *Denial of Violence: Ottoman Past, Turkish Present, and Collective Violence against the Armenians, 1789–2009* (Oxford University Press, 2015). She is currently working on two book projects: *The Kurdish Genocide in the Turkish Republic* (with Adnan Celik), based on sixty interviews; and *Foundational Vectors of Violence in the United States: The Native American and African American Genocides.*

SANDRA LEATON GRAY, University College London, England
Professor Sandra Leaton Gray is professor of education futures at the UCL Institute of Education and has been a doctoral supervisor for sixteen years. She is a sociology of education specialist, with a special interest in issues surrounding the ethics of artificial intelligence, identity, technology, and surveillance. Sandra is also a member of the Privacy Expert Group of the Biometrics Institute, and chair of the Artificial and Human Intelligence Group of the British Educational Research Association. Sandra is the author of several books on education, including *Teachers under Siege; Invisibly Blighted: The Digital Erosion of Childhood; Digital Children: A Guide for Adults; Curriculum Reform in the European Schools; Women Curriculum Theorists; Intelligence, Sapience and Learning*; and *Colonising and Decolonising: Concepts, Learnings and Praxes.*

MATHEW GUEST, Durham University, England
Dr. Mathew Guest is professor in the sociology of religion, Department of Theology and Religion, Durham University, UK. He has published a range of books, articles, and essays on evangelical Christianity, religion and generational change, the negotiation of religious identities within higher education, and the neoliberal forms of contemporary religion. He has taught at Durham University since 2004, where he has supervised thirty-two postgraduate research students and examined another nineteen across a range of universities. He has been his department's

Director of Postgraduates (2013–17) and was one of three recipients of the university's Award for Excellence in Doctoral Supervision in 2011.

CELIA HAIG-BROWN, York University, Canada

Celia Haig-Brown, Fellow of the Royal Society of Canada, is Professor Emerita/Senior Scholar at York University. Anglo-Canadian, she is committed to respectful and reciprocal research working with Indigenous collaborators from Secwépemc territory to the Naskapi Nation. Her 1988 book, based on testimonies of residential school survivors, was revised with Indigenous contributors and published in 2022: *Tsqelmucwílc: The Kamloops Indian Residential School: Resistance and a Reckoning*. She has supervised eighteen doctoral students, all of whom have served as professors, administrators, and education specialists in universities, colleges, and industry. In 2016, she won York's Faculty of Graduate Studies Teaching Award.

RANDY ALLEN HARRIS, University of Waterloo, Canada

Randy Allen Harris studies rhetoric, linguistics, and computational stylistics. His favorite recurrent hallway encounter was with a doctoral student (let's call him "Adam Bradley"), who always responded to his query, "How is it going, Adam?" with "Living the dream, Dr. H. Living the dream."

ANDREW HAYWARD, University College London, England

Andrew Hayward is professor of infectious disease epidemiology and inclusion health at UCL. His research is divided between work that aims to improve the control of infections (e.g., tuberculosis, influenza, and antimicrobial resistance) and to reduce the extreme health inequalities faced by socially excluded groups (such as those experiencing homelessness, addiction, or imprisonment). Andrew has gained many valued colleagues through PhD supervision and is fortunate to have learnt more from his students than they have from him! He directs the UCL Institute of Epidemiology and Health Care and codirects the UCL Collaborative Centre for Inclusion Health.

KATHRYN HIBBERT, Western University, Canada

Kathy Hibbert is a Distinguished University Professor at Western University. She is cross-appointed with the Faculty of Education and the Department of Medical Imaging, at the Schulich School of Medicine & Dentistry. Being an interdisciplinary scholar has introduced her to a wide variety of students across disciplines and a range of ways to work together. She has had the pleasure of serving as supervisor or being on committees for ninety-six students and she learned something beautiful from each of them. Kathy was the beneficiary of the superb supervision of Dr. Sharon Rich, who was an expert at building community and leading with compassion and grace.

LAURIE HOFFMAN-GOETZ, University of Waterloo, Canada

Dr. Laurie Hoffman-Goetz is a Distinguished Professor Emerita at the University of Waterloo, Ontario, Canada, and a recipient of the University Award for Excellence in Graduate Supervision. She served as Associate Dean of Graduate Studies in the Faculty of Applied Health Sciences at Waterloo. Dr. Hoffman-Goetz holds a PhD from the University of Michigan (Biological Anthropology, focus on physiology) and an MPH from George Washington University (Public Health). Her guiding principle is that the specific PhD field matters less than curiosity and passion for learning, enjoyment in straddling often siloed academic disciplines, and belief in the community of colleagues-in-training in the knowledge quest. She has published two hundred articles and two books. She is happiest as a teacher and a student.

LEE HUMPHREYS, Cornell University, United States

Lee Humphreys is a professor and chair of the Department of Communication at Cornell University. She studies the social uses and perceived effects of communication technology, specifically focusing on mobile and social media. She is the author of *The Qualified Self: Social Media and the Accounting of Everyday Life* (MIT Press, 2018) and the coeditor, with Paul Messaris, of *Digital Media: Transformations in Human Communication* (Peter Lang, 2005/2017). Her research has appeared in the *Journal of Communication, New*

Media & Society, and the *Journal of Computer-Mediated Communication*, among others. She received her PhD from the University of Pennsylvania's Annenberg School in 2007.

LAURENCE HURST, University of Bath, England

Laurence Hurst is a professor of evolutionary genetics at the Milner Centre for Evolution at the University of Bath, UK. He did his undergraduate degree at Cambridge University, and was a Fellow for a year at Harvard University before doing his DPhil at Oxford University. After appointment as a Research Fellow at Queen's College Oxford, he was awarded a Royal Society Research Fellowship and moved back to Cambridge University. He is the recipient of the Scientific Medal of the Zoological Society of London, the VC Research Medal, a Royal Society Wolfson Merit Award, the Genetics Society Medal, and the Humboldt Prize. He is an elected member of EMBO, of the Fellowship of the Academy of Medical Sciences, and of the Royal Society of London. He is past president of the Genetics Society. He was also the inaugural winner of his university's prize for doctoral supervision.

JOHN JACKSON, University of Michigan, United States

John E. Jackson is the M. Kent Jennings Professor of Political Science Emeritus at the University of Michigan. His research contributes to US politics, empirical methodology, and comparative political economy. He has a BS and MS in industrial administration from Carnegie Mellon University and an MPA and PhD in political economy and government from Harvard University. He has taught at the University of Michigan since 1980. Before that he taught political science at the University of Pennsylvania and Harvard University and economics at the US Air Force Academy. He served on active duty in the US Army from 1968 to 1970.

PETER JACKSON, University of Sheffield, England

Peter Jackson is professor of human geography at the University of Sheffield, UK. After doctoral research in Oxford, he taught at University College London before taking up his current post in Sheffield in 1993. His research focuses on food insecurity and sustainability with a particular focus on the connections between families and food. He is currently directing the H3 project (Healthy soil, Healthy food, Healthy people), funded by UKRI's Transforming UK Food Systems program. Recent publications include *Food Words* (Bloomsbury, 2013), *Anxious Appetites* (Bloomsbury, 2015), and *Reframing Convenience Food* (Palgrave Macmillan, 2018). He has supervised more than thirty PhD students to successful completion.

ZOE JAQUES, University of Cambridge, England

Dr. Zoe Jaques is University Professor in the Faculty of Education, University of Cambridge, and Dean of Homerton College. She specializes in researching children's literature. She is the author of *Lewis Carroll's* Alice's Adventures in Wonderland *and* Through the Looking Glass*: A Publishing History* (Ashgate, 2013); *Children's Literature and the Posthuman* (Routledge, 2015); and general editor of the forthcoming *Cambridge History of Children's Literature in English* (Cambridge University Press, 2025). She has managed the doctoral program at the Faculty of Education and has supervised many PhD candidates. In 2019, she was named Cambridge University's Student Union Supervisor.

STEVE JOORDENS, University of Toronto, Canada

Professor Steve Joordens did his graduate work in cognitive psychology at the University of Waterloo, then did a brief postdoc at McMaster University. He is now a full professor at the University of Toronto Scarborough, and his research has shifted to the creation and assessment of educational technologies, especially those that support skill development. His work has won him a number of institutional, provincial, and national awards, including being named a 3M National Teaching Fellow in 2015.

BEATE KAMPMANN, London School of Hygiene & Tropical Medicine, England

Professor Beate Kampmann holds a Chair in Pediatric Infection & Immunity at the London School of Hygiene & Tropical Medicine in the UK and is the Director of the Centre for Vaccines at LSHTM.

She also serves as Director of the Charité Center for Global Health at the Universitätsmedizin Berlin. For the last ten years, she has also worked as the Scientific Director (Theme Leader) for Vaccinology Research at the MRC Unit–The Gambia, where she spends a third of her time. She leads a comprehensive childhood infection and vaccine research program both in the UK and sub-Saharan Africa, has published more than two hundred scientific papers, and participates in/chairs a number of international advisory committees. Prof. Kampmann has supervised eighteen PhD students to date, of which a third are candidates from Africa, in addition to a large number of MSc students and mentees. In 2015, she was awarded the President's Medal for Excellence in Research Supervision at Imperial College, and she received the MRC Director's Award for Inspirational Leadership on two occasions. She is deeply committed to developing scientists and clinicians wherever they are, and she works in partnerships with her trainees to further enhance leadership of African scientists in particular.

PATRICIA O'CONNELL KILLEN, Pacific Lutheran University, United States

Dr. Patricia O'Connell Killen is professor emerita and research fellow at Pacific Lutheran University, Tacoma, Washington. She holds a PhD in religious studies from Stanford University. Killen has published on Catholicism in the United States, religion, spirituality, and civic life in the Pacific Northwest, and on teaching theology and religion. She is an award-winning teacher and scholar who also served as provost at two universities. Killen worked with the Wabash Center for Teaching and Learning for nearly twenty-five years, including directing workshops aimed at helping new faculty to negotiate institutional contexts and thrive in their careers.

CLARE KOSNIK, University of Toronto, Canada

Clare Kosnik is a professor at the Ontario Institute for Studies in Education/University of Toronto. She holds a PhD from the University of Toronto. She has published widely on teacher education. She has held administrative positions at the University of Toronto and Stanford University. She has received many awards nationally and internationally for her research on teacher education. She was awarded the J.J. Berry Award for Outstanding Doctoral Supervision at the University of Toronto.

CHARLIE KURTH, Clemson University, United States

Charlie Kurth is professor of philosophy in the Department of Philosophy and Religion at Clemson University. He has also taught at Western Michigan University, Washington University in St. Louis, and the University of California San Diego. His research focuses on issues at the intersection of ethics, emotion theory, and moral psychology. He is the author of two books: *The Anxious Mind: An Investigation into the Varieties and Virtues of Anxiety* (MIT Press, 2018) and *Emotion* (Routledge, 2022). Kurth is an award-winning teacher and leads a variety of outreach initiatives for high school students, including the WMU Lyceum, a philosophy-oriented summer camp, as well as a philosophy club.

WINNIFRED R. LOUIS, University of Queensland, Australia

Winnifred R. Louis (PhD, McGill, 2001) is a professor in psychology at the University of Queensland, who has won university and international awards for mentoring and supervision. Her research interests focus on the influence of identity and norms on social decision-making. She has studied this broad topic in contexts from political activism to peace psychology to health and the environment.

BRUCE MACDONALD, University of Auckland, New Zealand

Bruce's long-term goal is to design intelligent robotic assistants that improve the quality of people's lives, with primary research interests in human-robot interaction and robot programming systems, and applications in areas such as healthcare and agriculture. He studied in Christchurch, New Zealand, taught in Calgary, Canada, and returned to New Zealand to Auckland, and is now the director of the department's robotics group and the leader for the multidisciplinary CARES robotics center at the University of Auckland. He is vice-chairman and founder of New Zealand's robotics, automation, and sensing association, NZRAS.

For New Zealand's national science challenge, Science for Technological Innovation, he is the theme leader for Sensors, Robotics, and Automation, and deputy director.

KAREN E. MAKUCH, Imperial College London, England

Karen is senior lecturer (associate professor) in environmental law at the Centre for Environmental Policy, Imperial College, London, UK. She is course convenor for the Global Environmental Change and Policy Option of the Master's Degree in Environmental Technology. Karen runs the Makuch Doctoral Research Group. She is the former Faculty of Natural Sciences Ambassador for Women. Among other things, Karen is the recipient of the Imperial College President's Award for Excellence in Research Supervision, Imperial College London, 2018; the Imperial College London Faculty of Natural Sciences Award winner for Excellence in the Support of Teaching and Learning, 2016; and the Julia Higgins Award winner for Support of Academic Women, Imperial College London, 2015. Karen has research interests in the environmental rights of children, environmental law and policy, international environmental law (including human rights and climate "justice"), public interest environmental law (including access to environmental information and public participation), gender and environment, citizen science, and the role that law can play in regulating science and technology. She is dedicated to her students, to equality and diversity, and to making the world a better place through everything she does.

JOCELYNE MATHIEU, Université Laval, Canada

Jocelyne Mathieu holds a doctorate in ethnology from L'École des hautes études en sciences sociales in Paris. Until 2023, she was a titular professor in the Département des sciences historiques at Université Laval. Some of her areas of expertise include material culture, Quebecois and Euro-American customs, daily and domestic life, costumes and fashion, handcrafted textiles, popular arts, and regional identity. Especially interested in the relationship between tradition and fashion, as well as women's education, she favors research in the field and in archives. She is a member of La Société des Dix and publishes annually in *Les cahiers des Dix.*

CHERYL MCEWAN, Durham University, England

Cheryl McEwan is professor of human geography at Durham University in the UK. A specialist in cultural, postcolonial, and feminist geographies, she has supervised over thirty PhD theses. Cheryl's approach to supervision is as critical friend in a non-hierarchical, mutually supportive relationship based on trust, honesty, and free exchange of ideas. Working with a diverse group of doctoral researchers has taught her that there is no single model of supervision since individuals respond in different ways to the demands of research and the intellectual environment they inhabit. However, encouragement, appropriate support, and building confidence and independence are essential to success.

JASON METCALFE, University of North Carolina at Chapel Hill, United States

Jason Metcalfe is a professor in the Department of Mathematics at the University of North Carolina at Chapel Hill (UNC). He received his PhD from Johns Hopkins University. Metcalfe is the recipient of multiple teaching and mentoring awards including the 2018 Board of Governors' Award for Excellence in Teaching from the UNC System and the 2019 Faculty Award for Excellence in Doctoral Mentoring from the Graduate School at UNC.

JAMES MOODY, Duke University, United States

James Moody is professor of sociology at Duke University and founding director of the Duke Network Analysis Center. He has published extensively in the field of social networks, methods, and social theory with over eighty peer-reviewed papers and extensive applied consultation with industry and the US Department of Defense. His work has focused theoretically on the network foundations of social cohesion and diffusion, with a particular emphasis on building tools and methods for understanding dynamic social networks. He has used network models to help understand organizational performance, school racial segregation, adolescent health, disease spread, economic development, and the development of scientific disciplines (among others).

ROGER MOORE, St. Thomas University, Canada

Emeritus professor Dr. Roger Moore (BA, Bristol; MA, PhD, Toronto), taught at St. Thomas University from 1972 to 2009. In 1996, he received the St. Thomas University Special Merit Award for Research along with the first STU Excellence in Teaching Award. In 1997, he received the Distinguished Teacher Award from the Association of Atlantic Universities, and in 2000, the prestigious 3M Teaching Fellowship. He is an award-winning creative writer (poetry and prose), rugby coach, teacher, and scholar.

ANNE EAKIN MOSS, University of Chicago, United States

Anne Eakin Moss is associate professor in the Department of Slavic Languages and Literatures at the University of Chicago, where she is also resource faculty in cinema and media studies and the Center for the Study of Gender and Sexuality. She is the author of *Only Among Women: Philosophies of Community in the Russian Imagination, 1860–1940* (Northwestern University Press, 2020) and numerous articles on Soviet cinema. Formerly a professor in the Department of Comparative Thought and Literature at Johns Hopkins University, she was awarded the JHU Krieger School of Arts and Sciences Graduate Teaching/Mentoring Award in 2017.

RAM MURTY, Queen's University, Canada

M. Ram Murty obtained his PhD from MIT (1980) and then held postdoctoral fellowships at IAS (Princeton) and TIFR (Mumbai). He was a professor at McGill University (1982–1996), and now is Queen's Research Chair and A.V. Douglas Distinguished University Professor at Queen's University. He was awarded the Coxeter-James Prize (1988), Balaguer Prize (1996), Jeffery-Williams Prize (2003), Queen's Research Prize (2003), and elected Fellow of the Royal Society of Canada (1990), Fields Institute (2003), Indian National Science Academy (2008), American Mathematical Society (2012), and Canadian Mathematical Society (2018). He received the E.W.R. Steacie Fellowship (1991), Killam Research Fellowship (1998), and the Simons Fellowship (2013). In 2018, he was awarded the Excellence in Graduate Supervision Prize at Queen's

University, and in 2024, the CRM-Fields-PIMS Prize. He has written more than 250 research papers, a dozen books, and supervised more than twenty doctoral students and thirty-six postdoctoral fellows. He is also cross-appointed to the Department of Philosophy where he gives regular courses on mathematical logic and Indian philosophy.

MAHMUT PARLAR, McMaster University, Canada

Mahmut Parlar is a Distinguished University Professor and professor of management science in the DeGroote School of Business at McMaster University, Canada. In 2013, he received the President's Award for Excellence in Graduate Supervision, and in 2014 his MBA students honored him with the DeGroote School of Business Dr. S.J. Basu Teaching Award. He received the Canadian Operational Research Society's Lifetime Award of Merit in 2018.

He has a BSc degree in mathematics and MSc degree in operations research, both from the Middle East Technical University, Turkey, and a PhD in management sciences from the University of Waterloo, Canada.

ELIZABETH R. PETERSON, University of Auckland, New Zealand

Dr. Elizabeth R. Peterson is an associate professor in the School of Psychology at the University of Auckland in Aotearoa/New Zealand. She holds a PhD in psychology from the University of Edinburgh in the UK. Elizabeth primarily publishes research in the field of education psychology, looking at students' beliefs and conceptions and their impact on learning. She has received a University Sustained Excellence in Teaching Award.

ANNE PETITJEAN, Queen's University, Canada

Dr. Petitjean was born and raised in France. She was a student at the École normale supérieure de Lyon (France) for her BSc and MSc (under the direction of Prof. André Collet), infused with undergraduate research experiences. She then moved to Strasbourg (France) for doctoral research on molecular folding under the supervision of Prof. Jean-Marie Lehn (1987 Nobel laureate in Chemistry), before postdoctoral training on DNA targeting in

Prof. Barton's group at Caltech (California). Since 2005, her group in Queen's Chemistry Department has been researching molecular shape control applied to drug delivery, and drug design for cancer and infectious diseases.

GAIL PRASAD, York University, Canada

Gail Prasad (PhD) is an associate professor in the Faculty of Education at York University, Canada. Her research examines children's, youth's, teachers', and families' social representations of linguistic diversity, as well as critical, creative, and collaborative approaches to teaching and learning for critical multilingual language awareness in the classroom and beyond. She is a coeditor of *Multilingualism and Education: Researchers' Pathways and Perspectives* (Cambridge University Press, 2022). In addition, her scholarship has been published in English and French in journals including *TESOL Quarterly*, the *International Journal of Bilingual Education and Bilingualism*, *The Canadian Modern Language Review*, and *Glottopol*.

STEFAN RINKE, Freie Universität, Germany

Stefan Rinke is professor of Latin American history at Freie Universität Berlin. He has authored and edited more than sixty books on Latin American history in a global context and was honored with the Premio Alzate by the Mexican Academy of Sciences for his lifetime work. Since 2009, he has been the director of the first German-Latin American International Research Training Group, a joint doctoral program with leading Mexican universities. He is an award-winning doctoral advisor of sixty-one completed doctoral theses by young scholars from eleven different countries, a quarter of whom have won major prizes. Many of his alumni hold professorships at international research universities.

FREDRIK MØRK RØKENES, University of Bergen, Norway

Dr. Fredrik Mørk Røkenes is an associate professor in English didactics in the Department of Teacher Education at the Norwegian University of Science and Technology (NTNU) in Trondheim, Norway. He also holds the position of Associate Professor II in the Western Norway Graduate School of Educational Research (WNGER II) at the University of Bergen. He holds a PhD in English and foreign language teacher education and school research from NTNU. Røkenes has taught, supervised, and published on professional digital competence, computer-assisted language learning, and digitalization in teacher education internationally and in Norway. He has also worked with systematic literature reviews in graduate and postgraduate education.

MARIE-CHRISTINE SAINT-JACQUES, Université Laval, Canada

Dr. Marie-Christine Saint-Jacques SW, PhD, is a full professor in the School of Social Work and Criminology at Université Laval and the director of the research partnership Parental Separation and Stepfamily Living (funded by SSHRC), https://arucfamille.ulaval.ca/. She holds a PhD in sciences humaines appliquées from Université de Montréal. In the last thirty years, Professor Saint-Jacques has conducted several research projects in the field of family transitions and also in child protection law. She has developed diverse teaching activities for graduate students and participated in various university organizations dedicated to their support. In 2018, she was presented with Université Laval's Award for Excellence in Teaching for the quality of the supervision she gives to her master's and PhD students.

MARGARET SIMMONS, Monash University, Australia

Dr. Margaret Simmons, associate professor in BMedSci/MD, BA (hons), PhD. Margaret is Deputy Director at Monash Rural Health–Churchill (Australia), teaching graduate-entry medical students a social perspective on health, where she also directs a community-based placement program. She has coordinated qualitative social research method subjects and is experienced in medical education curriculum design and pedagogies. Margaret has nearly twenty years of experience in medical sociology and qualitative research. Her research interests focus on poetic inquiry, narrative analysis, gender, stories of home, and pedagogies of practice in medical education. Margaret won both the Medicine Faculty Dean's and Vice Chancellor's Awards for Diversity & Inclusion in

2020 as well as the Medicine Faculty Dean's and Vice Chancellor's Award for Excellence in Community Education Programs in 2024. She has supervised four PhD students to completion.

SRI NIWAS SINGH, Indian Institute of Technology Kanpur, India

Dr. Sri Niwas Singh is a professor (HAG) in the Department of Electrical Engineering, Indian Institute of Technology Kanpur, India. He was Vice-Chancellor of Madan Mohan Malviya University of Technology Gorakhpur. Dr. Singh received several awards including the 2013 IEEE Educational Activity Board Meritorious Achievement Award in Continuing Education, INAE Outstanding Teacher Award 2016, and NPSC 2020 Academic Excellence Award. Prof. Singh has published more than 550 papers in international and national journals and conferences, and supervised forty-three PhDs (with nine PhDs under progress). He has also written thirty-three book chapters, and eighteen books. Dr. Singh is a Fellow of IEEE (USA), IET (UK), INAE, IE (I), IETE, AIAA, and AAIA.

SARAH STEIN, University of Otago, New Zealand

Dr. Sarah Stein is Director, Distance Learning at the University of Otago, New Zealand. Sarah holds a PhD in education from Queensland University of Technology, Australia. Sarah has published on a range of investigations undertaken in primary school and higher education settings, all into aspects of curriculum, teaching, and teachers' understanding of their experiences as professional educators. She is interested in the teacher-learner-curriculum-discipline-institution dynamics in formal education settings. Her particular interest is in the multiple impacts that higher education settings have on teachers and teaching, and how teacher professional development can support, enrich, and enhance professional growth.

TAMARA SUSSMAN, McGill University, Canada

Tamara Sussman is a professor and PhD director in the School of Social Work at McGill University. Her program of research in the area of aging, end-of-life communication, and long-term care has provided mentorship to over sixty graduate students by involving them in her research projects, connecting them to other students and researchers with shared interests, and inviting them to participate in unique opportunities such as writing retreats, knowledge exchange events, webinars, and specialized research meetings. In 2019, Dr. Sussman received the Northeastern Association of Graduate Schools (NAGS) Graduate Teaching Award for her excellence in graduate student teaching and supervision.

PAMELA ROSE TOULOUSE, Laurentian University, Canada

Dr. Pamela Rose Toulouse is an award winning Anishinaabe scholar and consultant in Indigenous education and Indigenous cultural safety. She has over thirty-one years of experience across the education continuum from K to 12, post-secondary, and administration. Dr. Pam (as she is more fondly known) is a proud Anishinaabe-Kwe and member of Sagamok First Nation in Northern Ontario. She is the recipient of the Ontario Undergraduate Student Alliance Teaching Excellence Award (2021); Inspiring Indigenous Women of Northeastern Ontario Award (2019); 3M National Teaching Excellence Fellow Award (2015); Laurentian University Full Time Faculty Teaching Excellence Award (2014); and the Laurentian University Professional Schools Teaching Excellence Award (2013). She is the author, researcher, and developer of over fifty-five resources in Indigenous education and wellness (e.g., books, chapters, articles, curriculum, webinars, others).

RÉMI A. VAN COMPERNOLLE, Carnegie Mellon University, United States

Dr. Rémi A. van Compernolle holds a PhD in applied linguistics from Pennsylvania State University and is currently associate professor of second language acquisition and French and Francophone studies at Carnegie Mellon University. His research and teaching activities center on second language development, with specific focus on pragmatics, interactional competence, and qualitative research methods. When not engaged in his academic work, Dr. van Compernolle can be found running long distances around Pittsburgh, or biking or hiking on the Western PA trails with his family.

VEDAT VERTER, Queen's University, Canada

Vedat Verter joined the Smith School of Business in 2022; he is currently the Stephen J.R. Smith Chair on Management Analytics. Prior to joining Queen's, Dr. Verter was the Supply Chain Management Department Chair at Michigan State University for three years, which followed his twenty-four-year career at McGill University. Dr. Verter specializes in the application of operations research for tackling challenges in the public sector. His areas of research are service chain design, hazardous materials logistics, sustainable operations, and healthcare operations management. His work in these four areas culminated in over eighty-five research articles in leading refereed journals. He served as editor-in-chief of *Socio-Economic Planning Sciences*, an international journal focusing on public sector decision-making, during 2011–20.

VIRGINIA WALKER, Queen's University, Canada

Dr. Virginia K. Walker is a Queen's Research Chair in Biology and Environmental Studies at Queen's University in Kingston, Ontario. She was trained as a geneticist both at the University of Calgary, Canada, and at Cambridge University, UK. Her research concerns the changes in gene expression after cold stress in bacteria, insects, vertebrates, and plants, which is communicated in approximately two hundred peer-reviewed publications. She has won teaching and research awards, but one of her greatest privileges and a source of joy and pride has been her role as supervisor to more than forty graduate students who have found satisfying careers in academia, industry, research, and professional positions.

CAROLINE WALKER-GLEAVES, Newcastle University, England

Professor Caroline Walker-Gleaves is professor of education at Newcastle University, Newcastle upon Tyne, UK. She holds a PhD in pedagogic praxis from the University of Leicester. Walker-Gleaves has published on teachers' decision-making and how this is shaped by their beliefs, together with teachers' life histories and the defining experiences and turning points that makes teachers who they are. Walker-Gleaves is a multi-award-winning teacher and scholar who has taught and researched at three universities and served variously as Provost for Students, Director of Research Ethics, and Dean of Education and Language Sciences.

ANN WALTNER, University of Minnesota, United States
Ann Waltner is professor of history and chair of the Department of History at the University of Minnesota. She has served two terms as Director of Graduate Studies and was the interim Dean for the College of Liberal Arts from 2023 to 2024. She was the founding director of the Institute for Advanced Study at the University of Minnesota. She has published widely in early modern Chinese and comparative history. Talking to graduate students about their work is one of her favorite parts of her job. She is currently working on a project on the reception of the eighteenth-century Chinese novel *Dream of the Red Chamber*, which can be found at z.umn.edu/Redchamber.

JUDY WIENER, University of Toronto, Canada
Judy Wiener is professor emerita of school and clinical child psychology at OISE/University of Toronto where she received the J.J. Berry Smith Award for Graduate Supervision. Her primary clinical expertise is assessment and psychosocial interventions with children and adolescents with learning disabilities and ADHD. She has conducted research on their self-perceptions, family and peer relationships, and the efficacy of school-based and mindfulness interventions on their self-perceptions, social skills, and relationships. She has published over one hundred book chapters and journal articles and coauthored a book entitled *Psychological Assessment of Culturally and Linguistically Diverse Children and Adolescents: A Practitioner's Guide*. She is currently editing a book on family and peer relations of neurodivergent children and adolescents, to be published by Springer Nature.

JILL WILLIS, Queensland University of Technology, Australia
Jill Willis is a professor of education at Queensland University of Technology, Brisbane, Australia. She researches the social structures of assessment and learning spaces to make recommendations for improving teacher and student agency. Jill is proud to

have led research on accessibility in assessment and student evaluations of vertical schools. She is a founding member of the Centre for Inclusive Education. Her favorite part of her job is working with her research students as they always teach her new things.

PIA WINTERMARK, McGill University, Canada

Pia Wintermark is a pediatrician, a neonatologist, and a clinician-researcher, specialized in neonatal neurology (https://www.neobrainlab.org). Her research program is at the forefront of 1) identifying as soon as possible the more at-risk asphyxiated newborns who will benefit from adjunctive therapies, using advanced neuroimaging techniques and bedside monitoring; 2) optimizing the treatment of these newborns during the first days of life; 3) developing novel therapies to repair their brain injuries; and 4) testing these therapies so to improve their future outcomes. One of her preferred activities is to mentor trainees, insufflating them with an interest for academic research.

LORRAINE YORK, McMaster University, Canada

Lorraine York, FRSC, is Distinguished University Professor in the Department of English and Cultural Studies at McMaster University, and a two-time recipient of McMaster's President's Award for Excellence in Graduate Supervision. She is the author of *Literary Celebrity in Canada* (University of Toronto Press, 2007), *Margaret Atwood and the Labour of Literary Celebrity* (University of Toronto Press, 2013), and *Celebrity Cultures in Canada*, coedited with Katja Lee (Wilfrid Laurier University Press, 2016). Her book, *Reluctant Celebrity*, which examines public displays of celebrity reluctance as forms of privilege intertwined with race, gender, and sexuality, appeared with Palgrave Macmillan in 2018. She has long dreamed of writing a book entitled *Unseemly*, and that's what she's doing now.

BONNIE L. YOUNGS, Carnegie Mellon University, United States

Bonnie L. Youngs (PhD, University of Pennsylvania) teaches undergraduates in French and Francophone studies for modern languages at Carnegie Mellon University, and has served her department as Director of Undergraduate Studies. Her teaching also includes teacher training as faculty and codirector of the MA program in applied linguistics and second language acquisition. She enjoys offering advice to anyone who will listen and was honored to win the Barbara Lazarus Award for mentoring in 2019. Her current research focuses on the use of AI to improve the learning experience for students, and how instructors can adapt their understanding of AI to improve their teaching.

DAVID ZINGG, University of Toronto, Canada

David Zingg is a professor at the University of Toronto Institute for Aerospace Studies, where he was the director from 2006 to 2016, and is currently the University of Toronto Distinguished Professor of Computational Aerodynamics and Sustainable Aviation. His research areas include aerodynamics, computational fluid dynamics, in particular high-order methods with the summation-by-parts property, and aerodynamic shape optimization. His current research is concentrated on applying aerodynamic shape optimization to the design of unconventional low-drag aircraft configurations motivated by the need to reduce greenhouse gas emissions from aircraft. Together with colleagues from NASA, Professor Zingg is a coauthor of two well-known textbooks in computational fluid dynamics. He was awarded a Guggenheim Fellowship in 2004, the J.J. Berry Smith Doctoral Supervision Award in 2016, and is a Fellow of the Canadian Academy of Engineering. Finally, at the time of writing, he has supervised forty-six PhD and sixty-three MASc students, many of whom hold senior positions in industry and academia.

Index